BIKER BILLY

Cooks with

FIRE

Robust Recipes from America's Most Outrageous Television Chef

BIKER BILLY

Cooks with

FIRE

Bill
Hufnagle

Whitehorse Press
Center Conway, New Hampshire

Foreword

THERE ARE SOME THINGS you can't fake. You cannot, for instance, fake being an astronaut, a fighter pilot, a brain surgeon, or a professional hockey player, and most certainly you cannot fake being an honest-to-gawd Harley rider, although thousands give it a try every Sunday in perfect weather. In like manner, you cannot fake the art of cooking or showmanship which demand proof of talent at every opportunity.

So, consider Biker Billy where those varied worlds of Harleys, gourmet foods and showmanship collide in an explosion of candy colors, blaring pipes, outlandish humor and head-warping habanero peppers. He's the real deal. When he talks of riding Harleys he means it. I've ridden with Billy across the southeast part of these United States, and he rides long and he rides fast. There's not an ounce of poser in his motorcycle riding exploits or myriad on-the-road stories.

The same with his showmanship. Biker Billy has enthralled audiences from coast-to-coast at hundreds of motorcycle rallies, local television shows, and network television on Jay Leno's Tonight Show.

Behind the table of his mobile kitchen, he slices and dices peppers to the tune of rock-n-roll. He tosses salads and cracks wise, he blends and marinades. He bakes, fries, and sautés with the audacity and wit of Robin Williams high on. . . well. . . devil peppers.

But it's in this book that his real authority impresses. Biker Billy, for all his bombast and hard bike charging, is a genuine gourmet cook. No one in the world of stainless steel kitchens or backyard BBQs can match his expertise as chef of this unique American food. Yes, he concentrates his considerable talents on the hotter end of the epicurean spectrum, but he's all the more unique for that. Every recipe herein is a delightful and fiery proof of his gastronomical talent. From snacks to appetizers to entrees, Billy has gathered together an assortment of his favorite El Blasto recipes so unique that you'll not find their like in any other collection.

So, enough talking. Let's get to cooking. Enjoy.

Beau Allen Pacheco
Editor, Cycle World's Motorcycle Travel & Adventure

Preface

IT HAS BEEN A DECADE since this, my first book, was originally published. It has been a wild ride. It all started with a local cable TV show that I syndicated to several communities around the country. Within a year of the early 1993 launch of that show, the first edition of this book was under contract and on schedule for a spring 1995 publication. Just before the book hit the stores I appeared on the *Tonight Show* with Jay Leno, *Good Morning America*, and then a whirlwind of other media appearances. This was a series of life changing events. In short order I was traveling the country doing live performances at events large and small. Over the past ten years I have had the joy and honor to travel and perform for audiences from as far north as Toronto, Canada to as far south as Sydney, Australia. I retired from my first career of owning and operating TV studios in Manhattan and have been blessed with the delightfully fun work of being Biker Billy.

It is all thanks to you, the wonderful folks who buy the cookbooks, enjoy the food, visit the website, read my magazine writings, and

come to the events. It is always a great pleasure to meet you all on the road, share some laughs, fiery foods, and the camaraderie of motorcycles on the open road. So let me say a heartfelt THANK YOU!

In publishing the second edition of this book we have endeavored to retain the look and feel of the original edition while correcting a few typos. While I have published two subsequent cookbooks and am actively working on my fourth, this book will always hold a special place in my heart. These recipes are dear friends that still grace my table. I hope you enjoy reading and cooking from this book as much as I enjoy making your acquaintance on road.

BIKER BILLY

Cooks with

FIRE

Introduction:
How to Cook Like a Biker

START by putting on an apron. Position a trash can where it is easy to hit with empty egg shells. Warn everyone in the house that the kitchen is now under your control. Then reach for the hot peppers and bellow, "Alright, cook with fire!" Now that you are ready to have some fun, let's talk a little about biker cooking philosophy, or as I say, "Get that French gourmet out of here."

I approach cooking a little nontraditionally. That is to say, I am not a professionally trained chef. Furthermore, I could care less about following the "rules" of gourmet cooking. In some things, like yeast breads or soufflés, there may be some purpose to doing it the way of the old masters. But beyond basic food chemistry, the rules just get in the way of having a good time. And for me food is all about having fun. In your kitchen you rule, so no matter what some stuffy dude in a big white hat says, do it any way that works for you.

Do you ever wonder about a cook who is skinny? Doesn't their food taste good enough for them to eat? One look at me and you'll know that I enjoy the taste of my food. Don't get me wrong, I am not against eating healthy. I just do a lot of tasting. In fact, I am all for reducing fat and

cholesterol and I think fresh foods taste much better than processed stuff. But it comes back to fun: if you worry too much about what you eat, then food becomes another source of stress—not the soul-satisfying experience it should be. *Life is too short to eat dull food.* And health and excitement are not mutually exclusive concepts.

Cooking with fire is just like riding a motorcycle—there are some risks involved, but if you prepare properly and use caution, the risks are reduced and the fun is increased. For example, hot peppers can add a lot of zing to your food without burning you (see the section beginning on page 8, which is all about hot peppers). But this book is not only about adding fire to food, it is about combining different flavors, textures, and colors. It is about feeling free to experiment and have fun. When you stop worrying about "doing it the right way," cooking becomes easy.

The concept of America as a melting pot is very appealing to me, and I enjoy mixing the foods of different cultures when I cook. When we think of our individual heritages as opportunities to contribute the best we have to the melting pot, we all become stronger. So try combining something Mexican with something Chinese or Indian food with Polish food, or even some of those fancy French gourmet items with something South American. Have an adventure, take your taste buds on a culinary tour, discover the freedom of cooking American food.

On a more pragmatic note, let's look at some of my eclectic approaches to recipe creation. I often determine quantities more by form than measurement. For instance, say I need one cup of minced onion so I mince two medium onions and have a little more than one cup. What am I going to do with the excess? My attitude is, unless you dislike onions, toss them right in. Everyone has different tastes, so there is no absolutely correct way to prepare most dishes. I believe that each cook also adds some personal magic when preparing foods. The recipes offered here are starting points for your magic. Add, subtract, or change as you see fit—the worst (and best) you can do is invent a new recipe. If you invent something new, write me; I would love to try it myself.

A few simple words about fire. First, I use the words *fire* and *fiery* to refer to the effect that the active ingredient in hot peppers has on the taste of food. I have not ranked the recipes on a fire scale; everyone's perception of fire is different. After reading the section on hot peppers and trying a few recipes, you will be the best judge of how fiery you want your

food. If my informality seems inconvenient, try applying the most important biker concept: forget the rules. The amount of fire I include in each recipe is what I enjoy; you may want more or less fire. Since I believe that the fire should not overwhelm the more subtle flavors of a dish, you should be "safe" (no guarantees at all) trying the recipes as written. And you can forgo the use of the hot peppers completely if you so desire.

There may be some ingredients in this book that are new to you. Or maybe you have yet to find the recipe to try them in. Since I live near and work in New York City it is very easy for me to find just about anything. I have tried to use items that are available almost everywhere. The Sources section, page 245, lists some places to purchase via mail order, and you can always write to me.

It is wise to read all the directions before starting—this applies to cooking as well as motorcycles. I learned this the hard way the first time I didn't use a shop manual to take something apart. Save yourself from experiencing this lesson first-hand.

Eat Hot, Ride Safe, and enjoy Cooking with Fire. Alright!

A Peek Behind
the Dark Glasses

THE ROOM is lit by the bluish glow of the TV set. The aroma of homemade salsa and the sounds of crunching tortilla chips complete the atmosphere. The screen goes black for an instant, followed by the flash of flames and the sound of sizzle. A moment later a seductive voice beckons, warning that "Biker Billy cooks with fire." ALRIGHT, you have crossed over the edge and entered the strange back alley where motorcycles and fiery foods collide. During the next half hour you will be taken on an unusual adventure. Your taste buds will scream for fire, the television will begin to smell like onions, and your blood will pump to the rhythm of a motorcycle engine. When it's over you'll shout "Alright, cook with fire!" OK, so maybe I'm a little optimistic. I hope you will have at least enjoyed a brief escape from your routine—if so, you will also have gained a little understanding of why I love to ride motorcycles and eat spicy foods. One thing common to both motorcycles and food is that they are both better when shared with friends.

Many very nice people have told me how much they like my show. I would like to say thanks to all of you because your enjoyment is what makes the show special to me. Many of you have asked me about the

show, how it started, how I learned to cook and ride motorcycles, and how the two became *Biker Billy Cooks with Fire*. I will try to answer some of those questions here and give you a peek behind the dark glasses.

Let's start with riding. Through motorcycling I have found many wonderful friends, and we have shared many happy meals together. Bikers come from so many backgrounds and places, but despite often profound differences, bikers share a common bond. It is this special unspoken camaraderie that makes motorcycling so important to me.

I am a biker because of many things. Partly it is the bikes and the road; partly it is the sense of brotherhood. But there is also a certain inner voice, a need, which words can't totally express. I guess motorcycles are part of my soul or destiny. My first hand-built skateboard, assembled from a piece of two by four, a fruit crate, and a pair of old skates, was my first "scooter." My friends and I had a lot of fun going *"vroom vroom"* on the side streets of the South Bronx. When my family moved to New Jersey I got my first bicycle, a Stingray that was my "chopper." I used to pretend that my bicycle had a motor as I cruised around town.

When I was old enough to drive, I wanted a motorcycle. I was hell-bent on getting a bike. But since my mom had to cosign any loan or insurance policy, it was a car or nothing. My mom was cool, so even though I didn't get a Harley, I was lucky enough to get a Mustang. I was always raised with a lot of freedom and encouragement to be me, but that car was my first real freedom and the beginning of my romance with the road.

My mom knew me better than I did at that time. See, I was a little wild and I managed to find more than my share of misadventures. Even when I was behaving myself, people would manage "chance" meetings with me on the road. So in retrospect, I see that Mom saved my life then so I could later learn to be a safe motorcycle rider. Thanks, Mom!

Back then there was no Motorcycle Safety Foundation (MSF) or systematic way to learn to ride. Some friend would just show you the controls and offer some "advice." That advice was usually based on superstition, heard from somebody who once met some guy in a bar who had been riding since before the Bible was written. It was up to you to learn riding skills the hard way—in traffic.

College, a career, a wonderful woman (happily, now my wife), and an exciting TV production business followed in rapid succession, keeping me busy for many years. Along the way, I forgot about my desire to ride.

When my thirtieth birthday rolled around I realized I needed to get away for a little while and rediscover myself. I took a one-week trip to explore Maine. I had been there on a TV commercial shoot ten years before and I'd loved it. Maine had clean fresh air, mountains, and a dramatic coast, and it represented a real change from a New York City TV studio. I rented a big luxury car, tilted the seat back, and proceeded to drive all the way up the coast of Maine. One sunny morning while driving, I heard the sound of thunder. Then I saw two riders approaching on chopped Harleys. By the time they roared past I had had an epiphany. I found what was missing: a motorcycle. I returned home a man with a mission. With the blessings of my partner and soon-to-be wife, Rachelle, I pursued my dream.

But how do you learn to ride a motorcycle in New York City? What about insurance and parking? After months of reading every motorcycle magazine I could, I decided to try the Motorcycle Safety Foundation's Rider Training Course for Beginners. I took the course at Trama's Auto School in Queens. Thanks to Gasper Trama and Curtis Heiserman, I learned how to ride safely and be an educated motorcycle consumer (and you can do it, too). Then, to make things even more perfect, my wonderful Rachelle bought me the bike I wanted as a thirtieth birthday present. Alright, Rachelle!

Now I had to convince Mom that I was not on the road to ruin. As it turns out, she was behind me all the way. Her trust in my abilities and her vocal pride in her son the biker meant the world to me. Thanks again, Mom!

How did I learn to cook? Well, I went away to school. It wasn't until I arrived at college that I began to teach myself how to cook. One visit to the "dining" hall and I realized it was cook or die. So I started to cook for myself in earnest. At first my meals were bland and minimal, but I began to experiment by trying to make cheap food taste interesting. As I got more creative, my food started to improve.

After college I started to work in TV commercial production and I temporarily left cooking behind. However, I sampled the offerings of many restaurants around New York City—from small, cheap places to fancy places that ad agency budgets paid for. I tried a wide range of food styles and as a result developed a taste for variety. I now had the foundation for what would later become a real passion. I knew the joys of good home cooking, I possessed some basic skills, and I was inspired by the

vast diversity of tastes the world offered. But I had to wait a little while before I could pursue the call of the wild sauté pan.

Rachelle, my wonderful wife and director of my show, was also my partner in a TV studio called Vidlo Video (now home of *Biker Billy Cooks with Fire*). For the first years, running the business was all-consuming, but hard work and sacrifice paid off, and we're still going strong after sixteen years. When we were finally able to relax, I returned to the kitchen and began creating exotic home-cooked food (we had had more than enough of takeout). I found that cooking allows me to express and share my creative impulses.

Rachelle and I always wanted to create our own programs, but for many years we had been so busy providing production services to clients that there was never time for our own work. We finally agreed to set aside some time for developing ideas. Meanwhile, I was still cooking and riding and sharing both with Rachelle and our friends. I frequently cooked chili, which everyone enjoyed, and I thought for a while about marketing my chili. But while trying to find the time to start a new food business, the idea for the show was born. And the rest is biker history.

Hot Peppers

If you look around, you'll find hot peppers popping up almost everywhere these days, just like motorcycles. And you'll find them in all but two recipes in this cookbook. One exception is designed to assuage your taste buds if you misjudge your hot-pepper prowess. The other is a simple sauce to put on already fiery foods. This section will provide you with some basic information about hot peppers and how to use them in your daily adventures with food. It will also help you develop your ability to enjoy fire and avoid getting burned.

I don't want to scare you away from using hot peppers, but you should approach them with respect. Even the most lovely peppers can be dangerous if handled incorrectly or misused. We are not talking third-degree burns, but if you get some habanero juice on your finger and rub your eye, you will know why hot pepper sprays are used to stop muggers. Whether you are using fresh, dried, pickled, or frozen peppers, they can burn your skin, eyes, mouth, mucous membranes, and other sensitive parts of your anatomy. If you grind dried hot peppers into a powder, the

dust can burn you, as can the vapors from chopping or pureeing fresh or reconstituted hot peppers. So should you wear a space suit? No, reasonable caution and some soap and water will usually suffice for the quantities used in daily cooking. After handling hot peppers, wash your hands thoroughly using plenty of soap and warm water. If your hands have cuts, broken or very sensitive skin, or if you are using very hot peppers (like habaneros), wear disposable rubber gloves; but still wash your hands after removing the gloves. If you are going to handle or process large quantities of hot peppers, use heavy rubbers gloves, and use a dust mask if you are grinding custom hot pepper powders.

Many of you already love hot foods and regularly cook with hot peppers, so you may not feel the need to learn how to cook with fire. But I know many veteran bikers who learned to ride the old-fashioned way and were surprised at how much they gained from a rider education course. I don't assume to be the world's foremost expert on hot peppers, but I love to share what I've learned.

Why add a fiery dimension to food? Well, life is too short to eat dull food. It is the same reason that I ride: life should be actively enjoyed, not viewed from the sofa. I like life and food hot and flavorful, with some adventure thrown in for good measure. But fire should never be added as a substitute for flavor. Nor should the fire of a dish obscure the flavors of the most subtle ingredients. Instead the fire should complement the taste of a dish and create a new dimension of enjoyment. This means that while hot may be best, hotter is not always better.

But what is hot? Assemble a group of fiery food lovers and start a discussion about just how hot is hot, and you will discover the most controversial issue in fiery cuisine. Unlike bikes, where it is possible to judge with scientific accuracy which machine is the fastest, the *perception* of fire in a dish is totally subjective. There are scientific methods for judging how hot individual peppers are, and there is even a ranking system using a measurement called Scoville units. Although Scoville units are used to establish a relative ranking of hot peppers, it still falls to the taster to decide how hot is hot.

How useful are Scoville units for the home cook? If you know anything about motorcycles, think of using only the displacement of a motorcycle engine to judge how fast a bike will be. It is easy to see that a 1200 cc motor is bigger than a 600 cc unit, but that is only part of the story. The same size engine can be tuned for more or less horsepower,

and you've also got to look at other factors, such as the amount of weight being moved. Similar concepts apply when trying to gauge how much fire a given pepper will produce in a finished dish.

What do Scoville units measure? Hot peppers contain a chemical called capsaicin. This is the magic bullet that produces the sensation of fire in your mouth and on your skin. When the fire hits, your cells send a signal to your brain that triggers the release of natural pain relievers (this is why some people get a special feeling of well-being from a fiery meal). Capsaicin also acts to temporarily squelch the delivery of those chemical messengers, which explains why you can develop a tolerance for more fire. The amount of capsaicin in a hot pepper is expressed in Scoville units.

Scoville unit measuring was invented by Wilbur L. Scoville, a pharmacologist for the Parke-Davis Company. His original testing method relied on a group of human testers who assigned a Scoville unit rating to a hot pepper by a consensus of three out of five taste testers. Today high-pressure liquid chromatography is used to measure the amount of capsaicin in parts per million. From a scientific standpoint the new high-tech method is very accurate, but the test only measures the exact firepower of the sample being tested, not the absolute firepower of every pepper in that variety.

Hot peppers grow in a vast variety and in a wide range of firepower, with some varieties being very hot and others having just a little zing. Many factors can affect how hot a pepper is, including breeding, soil condition, geography, weather, and time of harvest. It is even possible for peppers from the same plant to differ in fire level.

So does this mean that cooking with hot peppers is like playing Russian roulette with your tongue? In Russian roulette you spin the barrel and hope you don't get a mind-expanding bang. When you cook with hot peppers you want a bang, but you don't want to blow your head off. Fortunately, risk management is far easier with hot peppers than with Russian roulette. First, it helps to know something about peppers, and what the various varieties contribute to a recipe. Next, you've got to understand your perception of fire and how willing you are to take a risk. Part of the fun and adventure in cooking with fire is knowing your limits and expanding them (this is also true of riding motorcycles). Remember, if you go too fast too soon you'll never find your limit; instead, you'll just blow right past it and go BOOM. So if you are new to fire, start

slowly; you can easily add more fire, but it is difficult if not impossible to take the fire out.

Picture two motorcycles, one with a big motor and one with a small motor. Which would you say is faster? In most cases, bikes with bigger motors are faster than smaller ones, but there are exceptions. A highly tuned small engine in a lightweight bike can be much faster than a big lazy motor in a heavy bike. Just watch a 250 cc class motorcycle race and you'll see how fast race bikes with small displacement engines can be. Hot peppers are more like those exceptional racing bikes. So don't be fooled by the size; smaller peppers are often hotter.

Imagine that you're in the local bike shop to buy a motorcycle. You look at all the different motorcycles sitting on the showroom floor, and the choices seem almost endless. From sport bikes to off-road, from cruisers to touring bikes, there is a wide range of options to fit every preference and style of riding. So too hot peppers, with each adding its own unique flavor and level of firepower.

Motorcycles come in so many different configurations because there are many different styles of riding. Long-distance touring is different from canyon racing or boulevard cruising. A "standard" motorcycle will do all three, but will not allow you to excel at any one. Generic red pepper powder will add fire to any dish from cookies to curry, but it will not add the complex flavors that you can create using individual peppers. Generic hot pepper flakes and powders produce fire, but little else. The wide variety of hot peppers creates an opportunity to customize your cooking with fire. So feel free to experiment and explore the wonderful world of fire.

Hot peppers are available fresh, frozen, dried, pickled, and packed in a sauce. Fresh hot peppers are still mostly a seasonal product, and the flavor and fire will improve with ripeness or maturity. Most peppers start as a green pod that ripens to red, yellow, orange, or even a brownish color (with red being the most common). Green pods are usually good enough, but most are much, much better when allowed to mature.

Frozen hot peppers are relatively new on the market; they retain many of the virtues of fresh ones. Hot peppers are easy to freeze at home, so if you grow them or buy your favorite ones fresh, try freezing them. To freeze them whole, wash them and remove any excess moisture. Place them in a single layer on a cookie sheet and put them in your

freezer overnight. Once they are frozen solid, pack them in dated zippered plastic bags. They will keep for up to a year in a 0° freezer without any noticeable loss of flavor. If you are constantly in and out of the freezer, or it is set to keep ice cream soft, the storage life will be reduced.

Peppers are commonly dried for commercial sale. Most types are air-dried in their native climate and keep well for about a year. This simple inexpensive form of storage has been used for centuries. Some varieties of hot peppers, such as the jalapeño, have a thick flesh and will not successfully air-dry. Instead, they are dried by smoking (a smoked jalapeño is called a chipotle). When you purchase dried peppers, look for whole pods that have no black spots or fuzz, which may indicate mold or rot during the drying process. Freshly dried hot peppers are somewhat pliant, and as they age they become rigid and brittle. They are still edible, but is best to purchase them when they are pliant. Their shelf life can be extended by storing dried peppers in airtight containers. Some peppers develop a different flavor when dried; this is especially true of smoked peppers.

Pickled peppers are delicious on sandwiches, pizza, and Mexican food. They are available in both jars and cans, and should be refrigerated after opening. The variety of pickled hot peppers is growing as peppers become more popular. In some places, pickled peppers are the only out-of-season alternative to fresh ones. The fire of pickled hot peppers can be reduced some by rinsing off the canning liquid.

The following listing represents the most commonly available hot peppers, but it is by no means a complete list. These varieties provide a tremendous opportunity to begin exploring the thrills of cooking with fire.

Glossary of Hot Peppers

As a general guideline I use the following firepower scale. This is based on my personal tastes and is not a hard scientific rating.

Mild	*0 to 2,500 Scoville units*
Medium	*2,500 to 10,000 Scoville units*
Hot	*10,000 to 100,000 Scoville units*
Atomic	*100,000 to 300,000 Scoville units*

The peppers described in detail below rank on my firepower scale as shown. No fire rating is given with each recipe, so you can use this chart as a guide. Remember that when you add several different peppers together, they combine to create a fire level that is higher than each pepper separately.

Mild   *Anaheim, 500 to 2,500 Scoville units*
ancho/poblano, 1,000 to 2,500 Scoville units
pasilla, 1,000 to 1,500 Scoville units
Medium   *cherry, 0 to 3,500 Scoville units (cherries can be*
   mild, but it is safer to expect medium)
chipotle, 2,500 to 10,000 Scoville units
jalapeño, 2,500 to 10,000 Scoville units
New Mexico, 500 to 10,000 Scoville units
   (New Mexico can be mild, but it is safer to
   expect medium)
Hot   *cayenne, 30,000 to 50,000 Scoville units*
de árbol, 15,000 to 30,000 Scoville units
guajillo, 10,000 to 30,000 Scoville units
serrano, 10,000 to 20,000 Scoville units
Atomic   *habanero, 200,000 to 300,000 Scoville units*

Anaheim: Now known as a variety of the New Mexico pepper family, formerly this was the market name given to most chile peppers of this pod shape. Anaheims are long (6 to 8 inches), blunt-tipped peppers that can often be found in their fresh green form in supermarkets or Latin groceries. In the green state they have a fresh garden flavor similar to green bell peppers, and they become sweeter when they ripen to red. The firepower level ranges from mild to medium (500 to 2,500 Scoville units). You can substitute any of the New Mexico varieties, but some New Mexico varieties may be hotter.

ancho/poblano: The ancho is the dried red form of the fresh green poblano chile. These heart-shaped peppers are 2 to 3 inches wide and 3 to 5 inches long. When dried they have a fruity flavor with a wonderful aroma. The fresh green poblano is excellent roasted and stuffed and can be used like an Anaheim or a New Mexico chile. The firepower level is usually mild, but sometimes they achieve a medium level (1,000 to

2,500 Scoville units). Ancho peppers have a unique flavor for which there is no exact substitute; however, you can use pasilla or dried New Mexico peppers in their place. The flavor will change, but the result will still be enjoyable.

cayenne: This type of pepper is most commonly sold as a powder called ground red pepper or ground cayenne. There are several varieties of cayenne peppers; the primary difference is in the pod size. I have specified the long slim variety in the recipes in this book. The long slim red cayenne pods range from 2 inches to 4 inches in length and are pencil thin, with a curving wrinkled shape ending in a fine point. Other varieties can reach up to 1 inch in diameter and are 8 to 10 inches in length. Since they are equally hot, you would want to adjust (reduce) the quantity of the larger pods to compensate for the size difference. They produce a clean, crisp flavor that has been called acidic or tart, but their heat is more pronounced than their flavor. The firepower level is hot (30,000 to 50,000 Scoville units). You can substitute de árbol chiles, but the heat level will be lower. Also try the small red chiles found at Asian markets and sometimes called Korean peppers. To use ground red pepper as a substitute for whole fresh or dried cayenne, start with a level ¼ teaspoon per pepper used in the recipe. You will have to experiment because not all commercial ground red peppers are the same.

If you wish to grow your own fresh hot peppers, the long slim red cayenne is a good variety to start with. I have had success growing them both in the garden and in pots. They produce a good harvest, and the pods can be left on the plant until red with little risk of loss due to rot. They are excellent fresh and freeze very well, giving you a source of "fresh" peppers all year round. They also air-dry well.

cherry: As the name implies, these peppers look like large cherries when ripe red. They are most commonly found pickled whole or sliced in both the green and red stage. I also find them fresh in supermarkets and at farm stands. They freeze well, which preserves the fresh taste for cooking without the vinegar flavor associated with pickled peppers. Cherry peppers are good as a garnish on salads, sandwiches, Mexican foods, and of course pizza. The firepower can range from mild to medium (0 to 3,500 Scoville units); rinsing the pickled varieties will slightly reduce fire level.

chipotle: The smoked jalapeño pepper. Jalapeños have too thick a flesh to air-dry well, therefore they are smoke-dried. The smoking process produces a wonderful flavor that is quite different from fresh or pickled jalapeños. They have a delicious smoky taste and a hint of sweetness that is produced by the caramelization of natural sugars during smoking. Chipotles can be purchased as dried peppers or packed in a tomato-based sauce called adobo. I use both types in the recipes in this book. The dried ones can always be used as a substitute for the ones packed in adobo sauce. If the recipe calls for the dried ones and you wish to use chipotles in adobo sauce, a light rinse will remove the sauce (if the tomato-based sauce is undesirable). The firepower level of chipotle peppers is the same as jalapeños, medium (2,500 to 10,000 Scoville units); however, I have observed that the ones from Mexico tend to be more potent.

de árbol: In Spanish *de árbol* means "treelike," which describes the appearance of the de árbol plant. These peppers are very similar in size and appearance to the small varieties of cayenne, but they tend to have a straighter pod shape. They may be related to cayenne, but there is some disagreement among the experts. The taste is similar to cayenne, and they work well in the recipes that call for cayenne. The firepower level is hot (15,000 to 30,000 Scoville units), so if substituting for cayenne, start with the same quantity and increase if more fire is desired.

guajillo: These peppers are very popular in Mexico, and I frequently find them in Latin markets. They are similar in shape and size to New Mexico peppers, but a careful comparison will reveal that guajillos are more tapered and have a pointier tip. Some people claim that guajillos are also related to cayenne peppers. They can be used in place of New Mexico peppers, especially when you want more fire, as they are more potent. The firepower level is hot (10,000 to 30,000 Scoville units), somewhere between New Mexico and de árbol peppers.

habanero: The hottest pepper in the world. There are attempts underway to breed a hotter pepper, but the habanero is still the king of fire. These peppers should be handled with care and respect, or you'll get burned. I don't want to scare you away, but it is a warning worth ob-

serving. I love these little devils and use them in several of the recipes in this book. The fire from these is a real treat. Habanero peppers ripen to a variety of colors from yellow to orange or red, and their shape can be described as bonnet-, bell-, or lanternlike. The average size ranges from as small as a dime to the size of a half-dollar. They have a fruity flavor to them, and to me the fire seems to bloom on the palate as opposed to bursting. There is no substitute for habaneros, but the many related varieties of this pepper are marketed under different names such as Scotch bonnet, Rica red, and goat pepper. They are most commonly available dried or pickled, but I occasionally find them fresh at supermarkets, Latin groceries, or farm stands. They freeze very well, and I find that the frozen ones are easier to core without getting the juice on my hands (however, I always wash my hands thoroughly after handling them, and so should you). Habaneros are the definition of *hot* (200,000 to 300,000 Scoville units), but keep in mind that not every batch has the same firepower, so some will seem "mellow" while the next batch could be atomic. I have had good results growing habaneros—even one plant can produce a good harvest—but the peppers may be milder than those grown in a tropical environment. When using habaneros in a recipe, be sure to chop them as fine as possible (unless the recipe specifies using whole or in large pieces and later discarding). This helps spread the heat throughout the dish.

jalapeño: Jalapeños may be the best known hot pepper in America. They are a staple in salsas, hot sauces, nachos, Tex-Mex, and Mexican-style foods. You will find them available almost everywhere as a pickled condiment (whole, sliced, or chopped), and they can now be purchased fresh year-round at many supermarkets and Latin groceries. America is in love with jalapeño peppers. The dried version of the jalapeño is smoked and called a chipotle (see above). Green jalapeños are most common and have a crispy green pepper flavor; when allowed to ripen to red, the flavor is sweeter. They freeze well and maintain much of their fresh quality for cooking. Rinsing the pickled ones will slightly reduce the heat. I have observed that the range of fire in jalapeños can vary from mellow to surprisingly hot; the ones that come from Mexico tend to be hotter. There is even a variety of jalapeño called the TAM jalapeño that is bred to be milder. The firepower of jalapeños is medium (2,500

to 10,000 Scoville units), and they make a good reference point for most people when comparing the perceived fire of other hot peppers.

New Mexico: The New Mexico pepper comes in many varieties and was formerly called Anaheim. For a period of time this pod type was predominantly grown in California, therefore the name Anaheim, but since New Mexico is now the major producer of these chiles, the name has been changed. And the names are still often confused outside the Southwest. These peppers can be enjoyed in their fresh green state in salsas and salads or roasted, stuffed, and breaded. They are most commonly recognized as the beautiful dried red peppers strung into *ristras,* the edible decorations synonymous with the Southwest. Most varieties of New Mexico peppers ripen to red, but there are others that ripen to vibrant yellow or orange and even brown. These peppers add a full-bodied earthy flavor that most people will recognize as an essential part of the taste of Mexican-style foods. The firepower ranges from mild to medium-hot (500 to 10,000 Scoville units).

pasilla: In Spanish *pasilla* means "little raisin," and it is the name given to the dried form of these chiles. When fresh they are called chilacas, and you will rarely find them outside of Mexico and the Southwest. In Mexico the pasilla is a part of the trio of peppers used to create the famous mole sauces. The dried pods are about 1 inch wide and 4 to 8 inches long, dark brown to almost black in color, and somewhat wrinkled. They add a rich flavor with hints of fruit and smoke and an earthiness that is a welcome addition to foods cooked with anchos or New Mexico chiles. The firepower level is mild (1,000 to 1,500 Scoville units).

serrano: These bullet-shaped chiles are 1 to 3 inches in length and about ½ inch in diameter. Very popular in Mexico, they can be found here fresh or pickled in Latin groceries and some supermarkets. They are more common in the green state and produce a clean, sharp fire; when red they become a little sweeter. The red and green can be freely interchanged. Excellent in salsas and sauces, these chiles can be used to replace jalapeños when you want to add more fire to a dish. The firepower level is hot (10,000 to 20,000 Scoville units).

Biker Tips and Techniques: Hot Peppers and a Few Other Ingredients

GROWING YOUR OWN: Hot peppers can be grown almost anywhere that you have a good 120-day growing season. Indoor growing is also possible using grow lights. I have grown over a dozen varieties of hot peppers with good results. I enjoy the pleasure of cooking with fresh-picked peppers, and I have a large freezer filled with enough peppers to melt a small town. If you can grow weeds you can grow the hot peppers of your dreams. There is not enough space here to tell you all the secrets, but I am working on a book and a home video that will cover it completely, so stay tuned.

USING DRIED PEPPERS IN PLACE OF FRESH: Dried peppers must be rehydrated before you use them. In recipes that call for dried peppers, you will find "boiling water" specified in the ingredients with a reference to this tip. Remove stem (and seeds, if the recipe says so) from the dried peppers. Place the peppers in a small heatproof bowl and cover with water that has just boiled but is *not still boiling.* Allow the water to cool for 2 to 3 minutes after it reaches a full boil before you pour it over the peppers. If you use water at a full rolling boil, the peppers may develop a bitter taste. If you are substituting dried peppers in a recipe that uses fresh peppers, use only enough water to cover the peppers; using too much water may affect the recipe. Cutting the dried peppers into pieces (unless the recipe calls for a whole pepper) will allow you to use less water. Set the peppers aside to soak until they are fully rehydrated (this usually happens in the time it takes them to reach room temperature, but in a cold room it could take longer). If you are in a hurry and want to use a microwave oven to speed the rehydration by reheating the soaking peppers, be careful not to boil them.

USING PICKLED PEPPERS IN PLACE OF FRESH: The main concern here is whether the addition of vinegar will affect the recipe (curdling cream or changing flavors). To reduce the effects of the pickling liquids, thoroughly rinse off the pepper with cool water. Sometimes a pepper will become filled with the pickling liquid. Examine the pepper before rinsing to determine if it is filled; if so, cut it open, then rinse. The rinsing may

reduce the firepower, so you will have to adjust according to your taste. The pickled pepper can be used as directed for fresh in the recipe.

USING FRESH PEPPERS IN PLACE OF DRIED OR PICKLED: If you are replacing dried peppers with fresh peppers, it is not necessary to rehydrate them with boiling water. You should therefore omit the boiling water from the recipe unless it is needed to rehydrate other ingredients (for example, spices or sun-dried tomatoes). When substituting fresh peppers for dried in dough recipes, you may have to adjust the balance of dry ingredients versus liquids. Fresh peppers can be freely substituted for pickled peppers.

ROASTING PEPPERS: The best way to roast peppers is to find a comfortable chair, a barbecue grill, and a perfect early fall afternoon. With that setup you can roast the peppers slowly on the grill while you admire the fall sunlight sparkling on your bike's chrome. But since that may not always be possible, there are other techniques you can apply to roast peppers. If you have an indoor grill (lucky you), use that, or follow this technique, which substitutes a heavy frying pan and oil for the grill. Use fresh Anaheim or New Mexico peppers if you are planning to stuff them.

Using the tip of a sharp knife, pierce the peppers near the stem. (If you don't put a hole in the pepper, it will explode.) In a heavy frying pan, heat ¼ inch of olive oil over high heat. Place the peppers in the hot oil and turn often. When the skins have blistered and browned all over (don't let them get blackened), remove from the pan and wrap in wet paper towels. Put the wrapped peppers in a plastic bag. This will steam the peppers, and as they cool to room temperature, the skins will loosen and slip right off. When the peppers have cooled, remove them from the plastic bag and paper towels, and peel off the blistered skin. Cut a slit in one side of each pepper and remove the seeds and core. If you are stuffing the peppers, leave the stems attached for easier handling. The roasted peppers are ready to be used according to recipe instructions.

GRINDING CUSTOM PEPPER POWDERS: If you enjoy sprinkling crushed hot peppers on your pizza, then you can find true happiness grinding your own hot pepper powder. You will become familiar with the flavors of the different peppers used in this book. When you find the ones that really hit the spot, try grinding them in a food processor, mortar and pestle, or

spice mill (don't use the coffee grinder unless you can thoroughly wash it—talk about hot coffee). Combine different peppers and, if you like, add spices too. Remember to wear a dust mask and gloves (goggles could help), work in a well ventilated place, and wash up with plenty of warm water and soap. Store the powders in airtight containers, and you are ready to shake up a little fire.

HOT PEPPER PUREES: Several of my recipes use pepper purees, some made from rehydrated dried peppers (for rehydration information see page 18), others from fresh or pickled peppers. In general I use one or more whole peppers in the puree to produce the fire level I enjoy for that recipe. Your enjoyment of fire is different from other people's, so your hot could be my mild or vice versa. Since peppers are a natural product, their size and firepower varies, even within the peppers picked from one plant, and it varies to some degree depending on what part of the pepper you use. It is therefore difficult to control the fire of a dish by merely using fewer whole peppers in the puree. What I find works well is to puree the suggested quantity of peppers and add the puree a little at a time until the fire is right for you. If you find that the dish is not fiery enough for you, next time increase the number of peppers you puree and add the puree to the dish until you are happy.

CONTROLLING THE FIRE: Besides using fewer peppers, there is something you can do to reduce the fire you get from each hot pepper. The part that produces the fire is most concentrated in the fleshy center of the pepper, which holds the seeds, and the seeds by contact also contain a lot of fire. Simply removing the seeds and the fleshy core will reduce the firepower of that pepper.

GARLIC: In many recipes I specify chopped garlic; in these cases I have used commercial chopped garlic from a jar. This type of garlic is very convenient, but it is not quite as strong as fresh garlic. Take this into account when substituting freshly chopped garlic. Chopped garlic from a jar will have a higher moisture content than freshly chopped garlic, so it tends to tolerate longer sautéing before it begins to burn. How well browned you like your garlic is a matter of personal taste. I like it well browned, but if you like it lighter, just add it a little later. Where I feel that fresh garlic is really best, I have specified the garlic by cloves, with a

cutting instruction if necessary. Finally, I love garlic and use it in large quantities—recent research claims that it is good for your health, and the best way to get the benefits is by eating it (a good excuse). But you may not like it as much as me, so feel free to use less.

ONIONS: Unless otherwise specified I use common yellow onions, but you can use your favorite variety of onion. I find that red onions can turn gray after cooking, so consider this if the onions are a visible part of the finished dish. I love onions and use a lot of them, but if you don't like them as much as me, use less.

SLICING, DICING, CHOPPING, MINCING, ETC.: I highly recommend using a food processor; it saves a lot of work and I don't think I could live without one. You can't totally replace using a knife, but much of the cutting up required in this book can be done with a food processor. With a chopping blade I suggest using the pulse function to control how finely you chop things. Please read the manual that came with your machine and follow all the safety instructions (this applies to any power tool). Also, when using a food processor to make dough, be sure your machine is designed to handle the heavy load this creates; I have burned out a machine doing this.

BEAN CURD: I find that extra-firm bean curd produces the best texture for the recipes in this book. You can of course use firm or soft if that is all you can find. Also note that bean curd and tofu are the same product, although I know some people who say "Ooh, tofu, no thanks," but enjoy bean curd.

PHYLLO DOUGH: Phyllo is a pastry dough that is rolled to a tissue thinness. It can be found in the frozen foods section of most supermarkets, and since it takes a lot of work and time to make from scratch, I always buy it frozen. Phyllo dough will produce a flaky golden-brown crust that is fantastic, and it is simpler to use than it appears. Phyllo must thaw before it can be used or it will crack. I allow it to thaw overnight in the refrigerator (check the package instructions).

Being so thin, uncooked phyllo dough will dry out and fall apart very rapidly if left exposed to air. The few simple guidelines that follow will help you achieve delicious results: First, the filling should be cooked and

ready for use before opening the phyllo package. The filling should not be too hot or it will melt the dough. Second, prepare your work area and have all the ingredients and tools ready. Third, unwrap the phyllo and cover it with plastic wrap and several sheets of moist paper towels. Fourth, remove only as many sheets of phyllo dough as you will use at once and re-cover the rest of the dough while you work. Last, in order to achieve a crispy golden result, brush the phyllo with butter or margarine (you can use any oil, but butter tastes and looks best) during assembly. It is necessary to use several layers to create a good thick crust; I use two or three sheets at a time and brush butter on each set before adding the next. The top or outer layer should be well covered with butter to ensure a beautiful golden appearance.

TEXMATI® RICE: This American-grown rice is a hybrid of basmati rice and long-grain white rice. Its flavor has hints of nuts and popcorn, and the aroma, like buttered popcorn, is enough to bring the hungry bikers in from the garage. I find that it adds a special touch to every dish that uses rice. The cooking time is shorter than basmati rice, and it is grown in America. A brown rice variety is also available.

MOTORCYCLING: Take an MSF (Motorcycle Safety Foundation)–approved rider education course. Safety is a state of mind that starts with knowledge. Maintain your skills, motorcycle, and equipment, and yourself. Get involved; join the AMA (American Motorcyclist Association) and your local state MRO (Motorcycle Rights Organization), such as ABATE (American Bikers Aimed Toward Education). For more information, see page 246. And, of course, have fun as you find adventure by riding, remembering to Eat Hot and Ride Safe.

Biker Party Treats:
Appetizers

BIKERS, so they say, are famous for partying. We've all heard the wild stories: bikers invade a small town, grab what they want, eat and drink everything in sight, and ride off into the night, leaving a path of smoldering ruin in their wake. Sounds like a B grade movie.

The reality is far different. Most big-time rallies (the official term for biker invasions) like Daytona, Americade, and the Black Hills Classic are major annual events that bring in millions of tourist dollars (and taxes) to the local host communities. In fact, the Black Hills Classic at Sturges, South Dakota, provides a large percentage of the community's annual economy. The most serious problems encountered tend to be traffic jams, parking problems, no motel rooms, and long lines at the local restaurants. When bikers gather in mass it is to have a good time, and to share good roads and good food with friends and family.

The big rallies are attended by tens of thousands of bikers and receive the most media attention. But there are thousands of smaller events each year that go virtually unnoticed. The BMW Motorcycle Owners Association (BMWMOA), the Christian Motorcycle Association (CMA), the Gold Wing Road Riders Association (GWRRA), and the Harley Own-

ers Group (HOG) are among the groups that organize rallies, and the events tend to draw a few hundred to a few thousand participants. On any Sunday in America thousands of bikers participate in small poker runs, toy runs, club rides, swap meets, parties, and charity fund-raisers. The groups that sponsor these events include the Blue Knights (police and law enforcement), the Red Knights (fire fighters), the Knights of Life (doctors, EMTs, nurses), and too many private clubs to name; and they often meet in support of local charities and community projects, some of which have come to depend upon the support of bikers.

Other than bikes, the one thing all the events have in common is food. Bikers do like to eat. The recipes in this chapter are perfect for parties and before-dinner munching. Give them a try and re-create some of the adventure of riding and rallies at your next biker party.

Many of the recipes in the next chapter, Salsas and Dips, can also be served as party treats or appetizers. The following recipes can be prepared as munchy tidbits as well:

Hot Garbanzo Bean Patties (page 88), served with Tahini Sauce (page 66)

French Bread Pizza from Hell (page 92)

Hot Smoky Potato Latkes (page 192)

Spinach Feta Fingers (page 198)

Howlin' Hush Puppies (page 218), served with Howlin' Cheese Dip (page 54)

Jalapeño and Cheese–Stuffed Beer Biscuits (page 223)

Remember after eating hot and partying hard to ride safely. Never ride drunk and never let a friend ride drunk. This also applies when using four wheels.

Spicy Bean Curd Egg Rolls

To many bike owners, a tune-up is a mysterious ritual best handled by bike shop pros. Many view Chinese cooking in this way. But these egg rolls are not mysterious at all. They have a crispy crust and a moist filling, and are easy to make at home. I use bean curd, but you may substitute pork, beef, chicken, or even fried eggs. Who knows? After you succeed with the egg rolls, you may be inspired to try your hand at motorcycle maintenance.

2 dried New Mexico peppers, stemmed and coarsely ground

7 plus 3 garlic cloves, minced

2- to 3-inch length fresh ginger, peeled and minced

5 scallions, minced

¼ cup olive oil

1 (16-ounce) extra-firm bean curd, drained and cut into ¼-inch cubes

1 broccoli stalk, trimmed and thinly sliced

4 carrots, peeled and shredded

1 medium zucchini, very thinly sliced

4 celery stalks, very thinly sliced

1 large red bell pepper, cored, seeded, and julienned

1 (16-ounce) package egg roll wrappers

1 egg, lightly beaten

Peanut oil, for deep-frying

Dipping Sauce (recipe follows)

In a small mixing bowl, combine the New Mexico peppers, 7 garlic cloves, ginger, and scallions. Mix until thoroughly combined, then set aside a heaping tablespoon for later use in the dipping sauce. (You may also use a food processor equipped with the chopping blade. Start the blades spinning and add the ingredients through the feed tube one at a time, in the listed order, adding each ingredient when the last is fully chopped.)

continued

Heat the olive oil in a large sauté pan over medium heat. Put the remaining pepper mixture into the pan and sauté for 2 to 3 minutes, or until the liquid has evaporated. Add the bean curd and sauté for 8 to 10 minutes, or until browned. Drain and transfer the bean curd mixture to a bowl; reserve the oil for making the dipping sauce. Set aside to cool.

In a large bowl, toss together the remaining 3 garlic cloves, broccoli, carrots, zucchini, celery, red pepper, and bean curd mixture. Lay an egg roll wrapper on your work surface with one corner pointing toward you. Place a scoop of filling on the wrapper just off center. Fold the near corner over the mixture, then fold in the right and left corners (like an envelope). Brush the last corner with the beaten egg and roll it closed. The envelope arrangement helps seal the egg roll, preventing oil from seeping in during frying. Place the finished egg rolls on a plate, keeping space between them so they don't stick together. Repeat until all of the egg rolls are formed.

Heat several inches of peanut oil in a deep pot or deep-fryer (see Note). Using care to avoid puncturing the wrappers, fry the egg rolls a few at a time until golden brown, 3 to 5 minutes each. Drain on paper towels and serve hot with dipping sauce.

MAKES ABOUT 20 ROLLS

NOTE: The egg rolls can also be fried in a frying pan. The oil should be deep enough so that the egg rolls are at least half immersed. If you use a frying pan, you'll have to turn them once.

DIPPING SAUCE

1 heaping tablespoon reserved pepper mixture from egg
    roll recipe
½ cup low-sodium soy sauce
Oil reserved from egg roll recipe

In a small saucepan, combine all the ingredients and bring to a full boil. Remove from the heat and set aside to cool. The sauce tends to separate, so give it a good stir before serving.

Fiery Vegetable Samosas

Rumor has it that in India, hungry motorcyclists have a wide choice among small family-run "fast food" stands, each of which offers many different tasty treats created with the proprietor's custom-blended spices. If only American fast food were so adventuresome. If you are bummed out because you can't take a year or two off from work to ride to India for a snack, cheer up. Just cook some of these Indian-style snacks to bring along on your next ride.

These tasty appetizers are easy to prepare, and the combination of a spicy filling and the deep-fried crust is sure to please the most daring biker taste buds. The filling can be prepared ahead of time and stored in the refrigerator. Allow it to warm to room temperature while the dough rests to ensure a warm center in the finished samosas. If you have leftovers, reheat them in the oven because the crust will lose its texture in the microwave.

Dough

2 cups all-purpose flour

1¼ teaspoons salt

¼ teaspoon ground cumin

¼ teaspoon turmeric

½ teaspoon ground cayenne pepper

½ teaspoon paprika

4 tablespoons (½ stick) margarine, softened

½ cup plain yogurt

4 tablespoons water

In a large mixing bowl, combine the flour, salt, cumin, turmeric, cayenne pepper, and paprika. Mix thoroughly with a wire whisk. Using a dough cutter or 2 knives, cut the softened margarine into the dry ingredients. Add the yogurt and blend well.

continued

Stir in the water 1 tablespoon at a time until a smooth dough forms. The dough should not stick to the bowl. Remove the dough from the bowl and knead until silky in texture. Return to the bowl, cover, and set in a warm place for 30 minutes.

FILLING

4 tablespoons (½ stick) margarine
2 fresh red jalapeño peppers, stemmed and minced (see Note)
2 fresh long slim red cayenne peppers, stemmed and minced (see Note)
½-inch cube fresh ginger, peeled and minced
5 garlic cloves, minced
1 medium onion, minced
4 small red potatoes, unpeeled, cut into ½-inch cubes
1 cup cauliflower florets
½ cup roasted cashews or almonds
½ cup golden raisins
1 cup frozen peas and carrots, thawed
½ teaspoon ground coriander
½ teaspoon ground cumin
½ teaspoon turmeric
½ teaspoon paprika
1 teaspoon salt
½ teaspoon ground black pepper
½ teaspoon sugar
½ cup water

Flour, for dusting
Corn or peanut oil, for deep-frying
Onion Chutney (page 65)

In a large sauté pan, melt the margarine over medium heat. Add the peppers, ginger, garlic, and onion and sauté until the onion is transparent, about 3 minutes.

Add the potatoes, cauliflower, nuts, raisins, peas, and carrots and stir

well to coat with margarine. Stir in the coriander, cumin, turmeric, paprika, salt, black pepper, and sugar, stirring well to blend the spices. Sauté, stirring often, for 4 to 5 minutes, or until the onion and potatoes begin to brown. Add the water, reduce the heat to low, and simmer, covered, for 30 minutes, or until the potatoes are fork tender. Remove from heat and allow to cool to room temperature.

Dust your rolling surface and pin with flour. Take a small piece of dough, enough to form a ball about 1 inch in diameter, and roll in a circle about ⅛ inch thick and about 4 inches in diameter. Cut the circle in half. Form a cone with each half by folding so that the cut edge overlaps itself. Pinch the edges to seal. Stuff each cone with filling and pinch the open end closed. Repeat until all the samosas are formed.

Heat several inches of oil in a deep pot or deep-fryer. Fry the samosas until golden brown, 2 to 4 minutes, then drain on paper towels. Serve hot with Onion Chutney.

MAKES 10 TO 12 SAMOSAS

NOTE: Cayenne peppers are hotter than jalapeño peppers. You can adjust the heat level of this recipe by varying the variety and amount of peppers you use.

Relentless Chiles

This recipe started as a classic Southwestern dish known as *chiles rellenos*. Then I got a hold of it and infused it with my own personal attitude. I call it "relentless" because, just like me, it's relentless and hotheaded. These babies are like riding a high-performance bike: once you experience real power and freedom, words can't explain it. You have to experience it yourself. Cook them, eat them—it's the only way to find the fire inside.

STUFFING

2 tablespoons margarine

4 garlic cloves, minced

1 medium red onion, coarsely chopped

1 fresh red jalapeño pepper, stemmed and minced

1 cup canned black beans, including liquid

1 cup cooked rice

Salt and ground black pepper

1 cup cubed cheddar cheese, in ½-inch pieces

TO ASSEMBLE:

2 cups coarsely ground corn chips

Pancake mix (enough to make 6 pancakes)

Olive oil, for frying

6 roasted peppers (see page 19)

Quick Salsa (see page 45)

In a large frying pan, melt the margarine over medium heat. Add the garlic, onion, and jalapeño and sauté for 3 to 5 minutes, or until the onion is golden brown. Add the beans and simmer for a few minutes, until the liquid thickens. Then add the rice, salt, and pepper to taste; stir

well and remove from the heat. Allow the mixture to cool to room temperature. Just before stuffing the peppers, add the cheese and mix well.

Place the corn chip crumbs in a wide, shallow bowl that is larger than your largest chile. Prepare the pancake mix according to the package directions. Pour the pancake batter into a large, wide, shallow bowl. In a heavy frying pan, heat $\frac{1}{2}$ inch of olive oil over a high heat.

Stuff each pepper with some of the stuffing. Dip each pepper into the pancake batter to coat and then roll in the corn chip crumbs. Carefully place the peppers in the frying pan and fry for 2 to 4 minutes on each side, or until golden brown. Drain well on paper towels. Serve with Quick Salsa.

MAKES 6 STUFFED PEPPERS

Hot and Sweet Dolmas

Also known as stuffed grape leaves, dolmas are a tasty appetizer, but most versions are seriously lacking in fire and excitement. Imagine riding a powerful bike that has been so poorly tuned that it coughs and sputters. Well, the average stuffed grape leaf has the same problem. I've tuned up these dolmas so they can take you to the heights of snack-time performance. Take your tongue for a fast ride through the mountains and valleys of Hot and Sweet Dolmas.

In this recipe I have used cabbage instead of grape leaves because cabbage is much more readily available. But if you happen to know a good source for grape leaves, substitute them for the cabbage. These dolmas also make an excellent side dish.

1 head green cabbage

⅔ cup plus 2 tablespoons extra-virgin olive oil

2 to 4 fresh long slim red cayenne peppers, stemmed and minced

4 large onions, minced

1 cup white Texmati® rice

2 plum tomatoes, peeled and pureed

2 tablespoons coarsely chopped pine nuts

¼ cup coarsely chopped cashews

2 teaspoons chopped garlic

⅓ cup dried currants

½ cup sweetened shredded coconut

½ teaspoon ground cinnamon

⅛ teaspoon ground cloves

⅛ teaspoon ground nutmeg

⅛ teaspoon ground allspice

2 tablespoons dried mint leaves

1 tablespoon dried dill

1 cup warm water

Juice of 2 limes

¼ teaspoon salt

Wash the cabbage thoroughly. Remove the outermost layer of leaves and set aside, then cut out the core. Place the cabbage in a large pot and add enough cold water to cover the cabbage. Remove the cabbage and bring the water to a boil.

Place the head of cabbage into the boiling water core side down (if necessary, use a wooden spoon to submerge the cabbage). Boil for about 5 minutes, then, using 2 large slotted spoons, pull the cabbage from the water and drain. When it's cool enough to handle, carefully peel off one leaf at a time. The outer leaves should be tender enough to peel off without tearing. When you reach the first leaf that won't come off without tearing, return the cabbage to the pot and boil for a few additional minutes. Repeat until all the leaves have been removed. Reserve 1 cup of the hot water that the cabbage was cooked in.

In a large sauté pan, heat ⅔ cup of oil over medium heat. Add the cayenne peppers and onions and stir to coat with oil. Add the rice and stir well. Finally, stir in the pureed tomatoes and nuts and simmer for about 15 minutes, or until all the liquid is absorbed.

Add the garlic, currants, coconut, cinnamon, cloves, nutmeg, allspice, mint, dill, and 1 cup reserved cabbage water. Reduce the heat to low, cover, and cook for 8 to 10 minutes or until all the liquid has been absorbed. The rice will still be firm.

To Assemble the Dolmas

Take a cabbage leaf and fold it in half along the center stem, using care not to tear the leaf. Cut away the thick bottom part of the stem. Open the leaf, and place a spoonful of stuffing in the center of the leaf. Fold the bottom corners over the stuffing and roll up the leaf. Repeat until you have used up the stuffing and large leaves. (Reserve cabbage leaves that are too small to be stuffed.)

Place a layer of small cabbage leaves in the bottom of a large, heavy-bottomed pot. Place a layer of stuffed dolmas atop the leaves. Add more layers of dolmas until the pot is full.

In a small mixing bowl, combine the warm water, 2 tablespoons of olive oil, lime juice, and salt. Pour this mixture over the dolmas and place a small oven-safe plate on top of the dolmas to weight them down.

continued

Cover the pot and cook on the lowest possible heat for about 1 hour, checking often. They are done when only 2 tablespoons of liquid remain and the cabbage leaves are tender.

Arrange the dolmas on a bed of cabbage, drizzle with the remaining cooking liquid, and serve hot or cold as an appetizer or side dish.

MAKES 24 TO 36 DOLMAS

Hot Party Nuts

No biker party would be complete without a few nuts. Since I like honey-roasted nuts, hot nuts, and peanut brittle, I decided to create something that was the best of all three. Serve these at your next biker party and your friends will go nuts.

> 2 tablespoons salted butter
> 1 teaspoon crushed red pepper
> ½ cup roasted cashews
> ½ cup roasted peanuts
> ⅛ teaspoon salt
> 3 tablespoons honey

Preheat the oven to 350°F.

In a small frying pan, melt the butter over medium heat. Add the crushed red pepper and stir well. Add the cashews, peanuts, and salt, and stir well. Sauté for about 1 minute, being careful not to burn the pepper flakes. Add the honey, stir well, and remove from the heat.

Transfer the mixture to a small baking dish and bake until bubbly and brown, 5 to 7 minutes. Check often to avoid burning. Remove the dish from the oven and allow to cool on a cake rack. Cut the nut mixture into squares with a sharp knife and serve.

MAKES 12 BITE-SIZE PIECES

Mexican Biker Turnovers

Oh boy, do I love Mexican food, and these babies are fantastic—crispy crust, beans, spices, and cheese. For me, a perfect summer Saturday is to go riding all morning, eat some of these turnovers, take a siesta, and then ride into the night. Even if you can't ride all day every day, you can enjoy these Mexican Biker Turnovers anytime, as an appetizer, side dish, or even a whole meal. I offer this recipe with two variations of dough: flour and corn. Be sure to prepare either in advance.

> **4 tablespoons (½ stick) margarine**
> **2 fresh serrano peppers, stemmed and minced**
> **2 medium onions, coarsely chopped**
> **2 tablespoons chopped garlic**
> **1 teaspoon salt**
> **1 teaspoon ground black pepper**
> **1 teaspoon ground cumin**
> **1 teaspoon black mustard seeds**
> **1 teaspoon ground coriander**
> **1 (19-ounce) can chickpeas, rinsed**
> **1 (19-ounce) can black beans**
> **1 cup water**
> **Oil, for frying**
> **Hot Empanada Dough (page 226 or 228)**
> **1 cup shredded cheddar cheese, or to taste**
> **Quick Salsa (page 45)**
> **Sour cream**

In a large sauté pan, melt the margarine over medium heat. Add the peppers, onions, and garlic and sauté for 3 to 5 minutes, or until the onions are golden brown.

Add the salt, pepper, cumin, mustard seeds, and coriander; stir to dissolve, and sauté for 1 minute. Add the chickpeas, stir well, and sauté for 3 to 5 minutes, or until the liquid evaporates and the mixture begins to stick to the pan.

Add the black beans and stir well. Sauté for 5 to 8 minutes, or until the liquid evaporates and the mixture begins to stick to the pan. Add the water and stir well to dissolve what has stuck to the pan. Reduce the heat to low, and simmer for 5 to 8 minutes, or until the sauce is reduced and thickened. Remove the pan from the heat and allow the mixture to cool.

Put several inches of oil in a deep pot or deep-fryer. Heat the oil to 365°F. The oil is hot enough when a small ball of dough dropped in the oil instantly sizzles and bubbles.

Roll the empanada dough according to recipe instructions. Place some filling and some cheese in the center of each round of dough. Fold the dough in half over the filling and pinch the edges closed. Place the turnovers in the hot oil one or two at a time (don't crowd them) and fry for 2 to 3 minutes, or until golden. Remove from the oil and drain on paper towels. The turnovers can be kept warm in a 200° oven while you prepare the remainder. Serve with Quick Salsa and sour cream.

MAKES 10 TO 12 TURNOVERS

Eggplant Puffs

In the realm of food, the flaky crusts found on Middle Eastern delicacies such as spanakopita and baklava are almost magical. How can any pastry be so thin and light? The secret must be complex and the technique incredibly difficult, not unlike the secrets of tuning winning race bikes. Surprise! Making light, flaky, Middle Eastern–inspired snacks is a lot easier than custom-grinding camshafts. In fact, it's downright simple. Just buy frozen phyllo dough and read the package or see page 21 for some biker tips. Cook up a batch of these golden appetizers to amaze your friends and family. If you don't tell them how easy it is, they'll think you're a genius.

> 4 tablespoons (½ stick) butter
> 2 medium onions, coarsely chopped
> 1 red bell pepper, cored and julienned
> 1 teaspoon salt
> 1 teaspoon ground black pepper
> 1 teaspoon ground cumin
> 1 tablespoon chopped garlic
> 1 teaspoon ground cayenne pepper
> 1 teaspoon turmeric
> 1 teaspoon ground coriander
> 1 teaspoon dried cilantro
> 1 medium eggplant, cut into 1-inch cubes
> ¼ cup water
> ½ pound phyllo dough, thawed
> 8 ounces feta or farmer cheese, crumbled
> ½ cup melted butter

In a large sauté pan, melt the butter over medium heat. Add the onions and bell pepper and sauté for 3 to 5 minutes, or until the onions are transparent. Add the spices and stir well to dissolve. Add the eggplant and sauté for 8 to 10 minutes, or until the eggplant is tender. Add

the water and stir well. Remove from the heat and allow to cool completely.

Preheat the oven to 350°F.

Place 2 or 3 phyllo sheets in a stack on your work surface. Cut in half the short way so that you end up with 2 pieces like the pages of an open book. Brush the melted butter over the dough. Place a spoonful of the eggplant mixture and some cheese on each phyllo half. Fold the right and left sides over the filling and brush the dough with more butter. Roll the dough toward you and brush the outside with more butter. The rolled puffs should look like egg rolls. Place the puffs on a baking sheet about 1 inch apart and bake for 15 to 20 minutes, or until golden brown.

MAKES 10 TO 12 PUFFS

Salsas and Dips

IS A BIKER without a bike a biker? This is one of those questions that can get a bunch of hard-core riders into a discussion deeper and more filled with psycho-speculation than a debate on theories about the beginning of the universe. I haven't figured that one out yet. But I have come to a conclusion regarding another of the age-old questions: Is a meal really a meal without salsa? The answer is a resounding no! If there is no salsa, it's not a real meal. But the recipes here may challenge your salsa preconceptions.

Salsas are easy to make, and they taste better if you make them yourself. There is no mystery—start with basic quality ingredients, and experiment. Adjust the fire level to suit your taste by either varying the type of pepper or the quantity (see pages 8–17 on hot peppers). I enjoy mixing a variety of peppers to find new flavor combinations.

Fresh salsas taste best after spending a night in the refrigerator; this gives the flavors a chance to blend. Believe me, when the flavors are well blended, they blend well with your taste buds. Another thing to keep in mind is that when an uncooked salsa rests, the heat level increases some. Remember this when adding your hot peppers.

Once upon a time dips were limited in their cultural possibilities. They could be sour cream or yogurt-flavored with onion or maybe bacon. And then there was (and regretfully still is) some pre-mixed plastic stuff that sits forever among the bags of chips, waiting for the unsuspecting dipper to come along. Now, thankfully, dips have been liberated and we can all enjoy a little freedom of expression. Let the dip recipes here get you started, then begin inventing your own favorites (and send them in to the Biker Billy Cooks with Fire Viewer Recipe Contest).

What chips should you use? Anything goes, so pick your chips (or what have you) and dig into these tasty recipes.

Quick Salsa

This is probably the great ancestor of all biker recipes; yes, salsa is not an invention of the nineties. Today salsa is everywhere. It seems like there are hundreds of commercial salsas on the market, each with a different taste. Around my house salsa is consumed with a passion, and I created this recipe to ensure a constant supply of fresh salsa to satisfy that passion. The key is to use quality ingredients and adjust the fire and spices to fit your taste. Experiment; salsa is what you make it. I use canned tomatoes because they are always easy and always in season, but you can use fresh. (I do when my garden is producing tomatoes.) Salsa can add a lot of flavor to almost any meal. It is also good to munch on while watching *Biker Billy Cooks with Fire*—alright!

> 2 hot peppers, stemmed and minced (see Note)
> 2 medium onions, coarsely chopped
> 2 to 3 garlic cloves, minced
> 1 (28-ounce) can whole plum tomatoes, coarsely chopped
> Salt and ground black pepper
> Dried cilantro (optional)

In a large mixing bowl, combine the peppers, onions, garlic, and tomatoes. Stir well. Add salt, black pepper, and cilantro to taste. Refrigerate before serving.

MAKES 4 CUPS

NOTE: Start with a small number of hot peppers (it is easy to add more, but it takes a lot of the other ingredients to reduce the heat). You can also prepare this in a food processor equipped with a chopping blade. Add all the ingredients except the tomatoes one at a time and pulse a few times. Add the tomatoes and process very briefly so you don't lose the chunkiness.

Cooling Cucumber Dip

Sometimes enthusiasm is stronger than reason, which can take you way past your personal limits. On a bike this can be a painful lesson to learn, which is why I am a strong advocate of the Motorcycle Safety Foundation's rider education courses. It is very important to know your abilities and to ride within your limits. The same concept applies to cooking with fire. This recipe for a cooling dip can help if you happen to get over-enthusiastic with the hot stuff. Keep some around to save those wanna-be hotheads who bite off more than they can chew.

1 medium cucumber, peeled and thinly sliced
1 (8-ounce) container sour cream (see Note)
Pinch of dried mint flakes (spearmint)

OPTIONAL

1 carrot, peeled and shredded
Golden raisins
Honey

In a small mixing bowl, combine the cucumber, sour cream, and mint flakes. Stir well to blend, cover, and refrigerate for at least 1 hour. Stir well before serving.

If desired, add shredded carrot or, if you would like a sweeter dip, some golden raisins or a few teaspoons honey.

MAKES ABOUT 2 CUPS

NOTE: You can substitute yogurt. If using low- or nonfat yogurt, bear in mind that the fat in the sour cream offers a soothing effect. This is because capsaicin (the ingredient that makes peppers hot) is fat-soluble.

Doubly Warm Roasted Green Chile Salsa

If you love the taste of roasted green chile peppers, this salsa is for you. As the name implies it is warm in both temperature and fire. If you want more fire, add a little cayenne pepper or a few dashes of your favorite hot sauce. After a cold winter ride I enjoy the double warmth this stuff gives me as it thaws me from within.

> 1 tablespoon extra-virgin olive oil
>
> 1 cup chopped roasted Anaheim peppers (8 or 9 medium chiles; see page 19)
>
> 2 medium onions, coarsely chopped
>
> 1 teaspoon dried cilantro
>
> ⅛ teaspoon ground black pepper
>
> ¼ teaspoon salt
>
> 1 cup water

Heat the oil in a small sauté pan over medium heat. Add the roasted peppers and onions and sauté for 3 to 5 minutes, or until the onions are golden brown. Add the cilantro, black pepper, salt, and water and reduce the heat to low. Cover and simmer for 10 minutes.

Puree the mixture in a blender or food processor equipped with a chopping blade for 30 seconds to 1 minute until no large pieces of pepper remain. Serve warm.

MAKES ABOUT 3 CUPS

Red-Hot Red Pepper Salsa

If you like red peppers, then this could be a drop-dead favorite. There are no tomatoes in this red rhapsody, so the flavor of the peppers comes through loud and clear. Add this to your Sunday brunch menu and you'll be ready to burn up the highways and byways.

> 1 tablespoon extra-virgin olive oil
> 1 or more fresh long slim red cayenne peppers, stemmed and minced
> 1 medium onion, coarsely chopped
> 1 red bell pepper, cored and diced (see Note)
> ½ teaspoon ground black pepper
> ½ teaspoon salt
> 1 cup water

Heat the oil in a small sauté pan over medium heat. Add the cayenne peppers, onion, and bell pepper and sauté for 2 to 3 minutes, or until the onion is transparent. Add the black pepper, salt, and water and reduce the heat to low. Cover and simmer for 10 minutes.

Puree in a blender or food processor equipped with a chopping blade for 30 seconds to 1 minute, until no large pieces of pepper remain. Serve warm.

MAKES ABOUT 2 CUPS

NOTE: For variety, substitute 1 cup diced roasted red bell pepper for the fresh bell pepper.

Yellow Bowl of Fire

Yellow is a hot August sun in the desert. The road invites you to ride—fast, faster. You feel the thump, thump of the motor as its heat rises to engulf you. The wind howls in your ears as the sweat runs into your eyes. Everything becomes a blur of speed and heat. Then suddenly you snap back to reality and reach for another chip full of this mind-bending salsa.

> 1 tablespoon extra-virgin olive oil
> 1 or more fresh habanero peppers, stemmed, seeded,
>   and minced
> 1 medium onion, finely chopped
> 1 large yellow bell pepper, cored
> ¼ cup water
> ¼ teaspoon ground white pepper
> ½ teaspoon salt
> 1 tablespoon golden molasses

Heat the oil in a small sauté pan over medium heat. Add the habanero pepper and onion and sauté for 3 to 5 minutes, or until the onion is transparent.

In a blender or a food processor equipped with a chopping blade, puree the bell pepper and the water for 30 seconds. Add the puree, white pepper, salt, and molasses to the onion mixture. Reduce the heat to low, cover, and simmer for 10 minutes. Serve warm.

MAKES ABOUT 1 CUP

Warm Tomato Salsa

While I love most fresh salsas cold, this warm version is a notable exception. The chipotle adds a smoky flavor. Consider it a new road to travel and enjoy the adventure.

> 2 tablespoons extra-virgin olive oil
> 2 chipotle peppers, stemmed and crushed
> 2 medium onions, coarsely chopped
> 2 tablespoons chopped garlic
> ½ teaspoon ground black pepper
> ½ teaspoon salt
> ½ teaspoon ground cumin
> 1 teaspoon dried cilantro
> 1 (28-ounce) can whole peeled tomatoes, coarsely
>   chopped and drained

Heat the oil in a large sauté pan over medium heat. Add the chipotle peppers, onions, and garlic and sauté for 3 to 5 minutes or until the onions are golden. Add the black pepper, salt, cumin, cilantro, and tomatoes and reduce the heat to low. Cover and simmer for 10 minutes. Serve warm.

MAKES ABOUT 4 CUPS

Hot Hummus

Hummus is a Middle Eastern spread or dip that is rich, smooth, and creamy. Pack it into pita bread halves and you've got the perfect saddle-bag sandwich. To make this a hothead bikers' delight, I've added some cayenne pepper and some extra garlic.

1 (19-ounce) can chickpeas, drained, liquid reserved

⅓ cup tahini (see Note)

2 tablespoons lemon juice

1 to 2 tablespoons chopped garlic

½ teaspoon ground cumin

½ teaspoon salt

½ teaspoon ground black pepper

¼ teaspoon ground cayenne pepper, or more to taste

OPTIONAL

Oil-cured olives

Pepperocini

Paprika

In a food processor equipped with a chopping blade, combine all the ingredients and ¼ cup of the reserved chickpea liquid. Puree for 1 minute, then scrape down the sides of the bowl and puree for another minute, until the mixture is smooth and creamy. If the hummus is too dry, add a little more chickpea liquid, or more lemon juice if you want a tarter flavor. (This can also be prepared by hand using a potato masher in a medium bowl. It requires some effort to achieve a smooth consistency, but the result is worth the effort.)

Serve on a plate garnished with a few olives and pepperocini. Sprinkle a little paprika on for color or use cayenne pepper for more fire. Have lots of warm pita bread available to scoop up the hummus.

MAKES 6 SERVINGS

continued

NOTE: Tahini is a peanut butter–like paste made from sesame seeds. It is the secret to the rich taste of foods like hummus, and there is no substitute. Fortunately tahini is available in most large supermarkets and health food stores, often near the peanut butter. Like natural peanut butter, the oil will separate and float to the top. Blend the tahini before using.

Chile con Queso*

At a party there are some dips that seem to last forever; then there are those that disappear before your eyes. This sinfully delicious blend of salsa and cheese is easy to prepare and sure to vanish. All things may come to those who wait, but don't wait to try this dip or it will all be gone. I enjoy this while watching biker flicks. So call your friends, grab a big bag of chips, and try this simple but fantastic recipe. One taste and you'll shout "Alright, Cheryl Maroziti, that's a winner!"

> **8 ounces cream cheese, cut into 1-inch cubes**
> **¾ cup Quick Salsa (page 45)**
> **1½ cups shredded cheddar cheese**

Preheat the oven to 350°F.

In a food processor equipped with a chopping blade, combine the cream cheese, salsa, and 1 cup of the cheddar cheese. Puree for 1 minute (stopping every 10 seconds to scrape down the sides), or until the mixture is smooth and creamy. Transfer the puree to a medium baking dish and cover with the remaining cheddar cheese. Bake for about 10 minutes, or until the cheese is melted and bubbly. Serve hot with plenty of corn chips.

MAKES ABOUT 3¼ CUPS

*Contest winner

Howlin' Cheese Dip

Back home from a long ride and you can still hear the wind in your ears as you close the garage door and head for the house. When you open the kitchen door the sound gets louder. It's not your ears, it's the sound of howling. As you approach the living room the sound gets louder. Carefully you round the corner and there's a terrific aroma. It's your family wolfing away at that fondue from hell, and they have saved some for you. Alright.

This dip is so good it will make your family howl, too. It is perfect for dipping Howlin' Hush Puppies (page 218) or breaded deep-fried vegetables. When the hush puppies are cooked, transfer the cheese to a hot fondue pot. Dip the hush puppies in the cheese and howl. You'll need a double boiler for this recipe.

> **4 tablespoons (½ stick) butter**
> **1 dried long slim cayenne pepper, stemmed and crushed**
> **¼ cup half-and-half**
> **½ teaspoon ground cumin**
> **½ teaspoon chopped garlic**
> **¼ teaspoon salt**
> **¼ teaspoon ground black pepper**
> **2 cups shredded cheddar cheese**

Fill the bottom half of a double boiler with boiling water not quite halfway. You don't want the top part of the double boiler to be in direct contact with the boiling water. Every so often, check the water level to ensure that the pot does not boil dry. Keep another pot of water boiling on the stove so you can add water if necessary.

Melt the butter in the top of the double boiler. Add the cayenne pepper, stir well, and cook for 1 minute. Add the half-and-half, cumin, garlic, salt, and black pepper. Stir well and simmer a few minutes.

Reduce the heat to low. Add the cheese a little at a time, mixing with a wire whisk or fork after each addition, until all the cheese melts. If the cheese dip is a little too thick, slowly add a little more half-and-half. (Be

careful not to add too much half-and-half, or to add it too fast, as the temperature will drop and the cheese will start to solidify. Unlike melted Velveeta or other processed cheese that comes out of a jar, this dip has a somewhat chewy texture.) Serve warm.

MAKES ABOUT $2\frac{1}{2}$ CUPS

Suicidal Guacamole

For years, every time I tried guacamole I thought it tasted like green slime. That changed a few years ago, when I took a cross-country motorcycle tour and visited a friend in Los Angeles. One day we went to lunch and I ordered a sandwich, which came with a small mound of guacamole. I politely asked the waitress to remove it, much to the dismay of my friend. After a small debate, she persuaded me to try the stuff again. It was so delicious that I asked for a side order of it. During that lunch I became educated in the secrets of guacamole. The main trick is to use only ripe avocados and don't try to store it, for freshness is the key. I call this version "suicidal" because I make it fiery hot with fresh cayenne peppers.

There are two varieties of avocado, a bright green, smooth-skinned Florida type and the dark, bumpy-skinned Haas variety. I enjoy the Haas. Peeled avocado will discolor after it is exposed to the air; you can prevent that discoloration by adding lemon juice.

> 1 or more fresh long slim red cayenne peppers, stemmed
>   and minced
> 1 small onion, coarsely chopped
> 1 medium tomato, coarsely chopped
> 2 medium avocados
> 1 lemon
> Salt and ground black pepper

Combine the cayenne peppers, onion, and tomato in a medium mixing bowl and toss well. Cut the avocados in half one at a time and discard the seeds. Remove the skins, cut the flesh into ½-inch cubes, and toss with the other ingredients. Squeeze some lemon over the avocados, and mash the mixture with a potato masher until you reach the desired texture (I like mine smooth, so I use a food processor equipped with a chopping blade to process the ingredients and achieve a silky smooth texture). Add salt and pepper to taste. Serve chilled.

MAKES ABOUT 3 CUPS

Condiments and Sauces

RADICAL choppers are the ultimate in customized motorcycles. But almost every motorcycle you see on the road is a custom motorcycle, even if it looks like box stock. Bikers are individualists, and we bring our individuality to everything we do, most importantly to the bikes we ride. Some riders go all out and completely rebuild their bikes, others just accessorize them. Total rebuilds can be as easy to spot as a classic sixties chopper, long and bristling with chrome. Others are totally stock looking, but have completely rebuilt engines and enough running gear to produce ultra-high performance. At the other end of the spectrum are accessorized bikes, which are dressed up to reflect your personality. If you ride long enough you customize.

Bikers bring this same individuality to food. Sometimes we want to fully customize our food so we start from scratch and cook it our way. Other times we want only to make small adjustments. While this book focuses on the more radical approach, this chapter is about helping you personalize your food.

Ancho Pepper Sauce

Some of life's most enjoyable experiences are found in simple things. It may be a freshly paved country lane that curves through quiet hills and valleys or the pride you feel after washing and waxing your motorcycle. Sometimes a favorite meal makes you remember special times. This sauce is one of my favorite simple pleasures. When there isn't time to prepare a special fiery dinner and I must resign myself to a burger and fries, I use this instead of ketchup.

This sauce should keep well in your fridge. However, it is best when fresh and is very simple to make. The ancho pepper is not tremendously hot, so if you want to make the sauce hotter, just add some crushed dried red pepper while you are soaking the ancho.

> 1 ancho pepper, stemmed and torn into small pieces
> ¼ cup boiling water (see page 18)
> Tomato ketchup
> Water
> Salt and ground black pepper

Place the ancho pepper in a small bowl and cover with the boiling water. Allow to cool to room temperature. Puree in a blender or a food processor equipped with a chopping blade.

Puree together equal parts ancho pepper puree and tomato ketchup, adding enough water to achieve the desired thickness (thicker for spreading and thinner for pouring). Blend well. Add salt and black pepper to taste.

MAKES ABOUT ½ CUP

Hot Honey Mustard

Some foods scream for mustard the way a sport bike screams for a twisty road. But mere commercial mustard, even the "spicy" stuff, is not wild enough for most hothead bikers. So give 'em the hell-bent mustard they scream for. This mustard is devilishly hot and sweet. You may want to fool with the proportions to suit your tastes.

> 1 dried habanero pepper, stemmed and seeded
> ¼ cup boiling water (see page 18)
> ½ cup honey
> ½ cup mustard, preferably spicy brown

Place the habanero in a small bowl and cover with boiling water. Allow to cool to room temperature. Puree in a blender or a food processor equipped with a chopping blade until the flesh of the habanero pepper is liquefied.

Add the honey and mustard and puree 1 to 2 minutes, or until fully blended.

MAKES ABOUT 1¼ CUPS

Biker Barbecue Sauce

What is summer without motorcycling and barbecuing? But as every motorcycle enthusiast has an opinion on bikes and roads, every barbecue fanatic strongly prefers certain marinades and sauces. This sauce is my favorite and I enjoy it on everything from burgers to vegetables.

2 dried long slim cayenne peppers, stemmed and crushed

1 ancho pepper, stemmed and torn into small pieces

½ cup boiling water (see page 18)

1 small onion, quartered

3 teaspoons crushed garlic

¼ teaspoon ground cumin

½ teaspoon dried oregano leaves

2 teaspoons salt

2 teaspoons ground black pepper

2 tablespoons Liquid Smoke

¼ cup blackstrap molasses

2 tablespoons olive oil

1 cup thick tomato puree

2 tablespoons distilled white vinegar

Place the cayenne and ancho peppers in a small bowl and cover with boiling water. Allow to cool to room temperature.

Briefly chop the onion in a blender or a food processor equipped with a chopping blade. Add the cayenne and ancho peppers and water and puree for 1 minute. Add the crushed garlic, cumin, oregano, salt, black pepper, Liquid Smoke, molasses, olive oil, tomato puree, and vinegar. Puree for 1 to 2 minutes, until smooth.

Place the puree in a small saucepan over medium heat. When it begins to simmer, reduce the heat, cover, and simmer for 10 minutes, stirring often. Cool before serving. The flavor improves if the sauce is refrigerated overnight.

MAKES ABOUT $2\frac{1}{2}$ CUPS

Hot Oil*

For a little edge without a lot of extra effort, this hot oil is just the thing. It was sent in by Lauryn Nolan and Jeff Carr, Viewer Recipe Contest winners. Alright! Use it for frying or to blast a salad to the next galaxy. I use extra-virgin olive oil, but you can use any oil that you like.

Always start with a fresh new bottle of oil and the prepared Hot Oil must be continuously stored in the refrigerator to keep the garlic fresh. It will keep for about one week in the refrigerator, please discard it after that or sooner if it becomes cloudy or bubbles begin to form.

> 1 head of garlic, separated into cloves and peeled
> 2 generous tablespoons of freshly squeezed lemon juice
> 1 (16-ounce) bottle vegetable oil
> 1 dried New Mexico pepper, stemmed
> 5 dried long slim cayenne peppers, stemmed
> 2 teaspoons ground black pepper
> 2 teaspoons ground white pepper
> 2 teaspoons ground cayenne pepper

Before assembling thoroughly clean and sanitize your work area and implements, and wash your hands. Inspect the garlic cloves discarding any that are soft, have spots, or bruises. Wash and trim the remaining garlic cloves. Place the garlic cloves in a small bowl, add the lemon juice, toss to coat, cover and set aside. Transfer 1 cup of the oil to a storage container and set aside.

Carefully stuff the New Mexico and cayenne peppers into the bottle of oil. Using a funnel, add the black, white, and ground cayenne peppers. Then add the garlic cloves one at a time, then use the funnel to add the lemon juice. Replace the cap on the bottle and shake vigorously for 30 seconds. Refill the bottle with some of the reserved oil. Refrigerate the oil mixture immediately and use within one week then discard any unused oil mixture along with the bottle.

*Contest winner

MAKES ABOUT 16 OUNCES

Cranberry Suicide Sauce

For a hothead biker like me, cranberry sauce never really did much for my taste buds, but it still evoked the Thanksgiving mood. I created this recipe to make cranberry sauce a truly fiery part of the holiday meal. Try it and you are sure to get a blast from the contrast of sweet and fire. It may even make your holiday memories that much warmer.

> 1 cup sugar
> 1 cup water
> 1 fresh habanero pepper, stemmed, seeded, and halved
> 1 (10-ounce) package fresh cranberries

In a medium saucepan, dissolve the sugar in the water over medium heat. Add the habanero and bring to a boil. Stir in the cranberries and boil for 1 minute. Reduce the heat to low and simmer uncovered, stirring often, for 10 minutes, or until the cranberry sauce thickens.

Remove the habanero halves and discard. Serve warm or chilled.

MAKES 3 TO 4 CUPS

Onion Chutney

This is a basic recipe that uses an important prepared Indian spice mix called *chat masala*. You can find it (and a whole lot more to excite your palate) at Indian grocery stores in most cities. If you have a hard time locating it, ask the owner of your favorite Indian restaurant; you never know what secrets you may acquire.

This condiment is perfect for serving with any of the Indian recipes in this book. The recipe will make enough to accompany a dinner for two. It can be multiplied, but let your taste control the cayenne pepper because the heat will increase rapidly.

> 1 medium onion, diced
> ½ fresh lemon
> 2 tablespoons salted butter
> 1 teaspoon paprika
> ¼ teaspoon ground cayenne pepper, or more to taste
> ½ teaspoon salt
> ½ teaspoon chat masala

Place the onion in a small bowl. Squeeze the lemon over the onion through a strainer to catch the seeds, and toss well to coat the onion. Set aside.

In a small sauté pan, melt the butter over medium heat. Add the paprika and cayenne, stir to dissolve, and sauté for 1 minute. Remove from heat and pour over the onion. Sprinkle the salt and chat masala over the onion and toss well. Chill, then serve as a condiment.

MAKES ABOUT 1 CUP

Tahini Sauce

While this simple sauce is not hot, it is so rich and creamy that it adds a new dimension to foods. Try it with the Hot Garbanzo Bean Patties (page 88) or any of the Middle Eastern dishes in this book.

> 3 garlic cloves
> ⅓ cup sesame tahini
> 2½ tablespoons lemon juice
> ¼ cup water
> Salt and ground black pepper

In a blender or a food processor equipped with a chopping blade, mince the garlic. Add the remaining ingredients and blend until smooth. Add salt and black pepper to taste.

MAKES ABOUT ¾ CUP

Breakfast and Brunch

MOST bike events are held on Sunday—not only is Sunday a prime day to ride but it's a great day to stop for breakfast or brunch. It takes energy and concentration to operate a motorcycle, and breakfast is a good way to fuel up for a long ride.

There are times when you and some friends will start riding real early and spend all morning enjoying the almost deserted Sunday roads. After riding for a few hours you will have developed an awesome appetite, and a bountiful brunch is in order. The recipes in this chapter will get you all fired up for the road. Remember the three important things: Eat Hot, Ride Safe, and Cook with Fire.

Kiss of the Devil Cocoa

This tormented recipe produces a fiery boost that will warm your soul and melt your socks. Kiss of the Devil Cocoa definitely is not for kids and is sure to surprise even the most jaded fire-eating biker. Try it if you dare, but be warned that you may never look at your mug of cocoa the same way again.

> **1 fresh habanero pepper, stemmed and seeded**
> **4 cups milk**
> **4 (3-inch) cinnamon sticks**
> **4 pieces Mexican sweet chocolate (see Note)**

Place the habanero pepper into a tea ball or infuser and set aside.

Combine the milk and the cinnamon sticks in a small saucepan over medium heat. Bring to a boil over low heat. Place the tea ball in the pan and stir for about 10 seconds. Taste the milk to check the level of fire. Keep stirring and testing every ten seconds until it is as fiery as you want. Remove the tea ball and set aside.

Add the Mexican chocolate, stirring well until the chocolate is completely melted. Remove the cinnamon sticks and serve the drinks in mugs. Pass the habanero-filled tea ball for those whose wish to soak up some extra fire.

MAKES 4 CUPS

NOTE: Mexican chocolate can be found in Latin grocery stores. It is usually packaged as a bar designed to be broken into pieces. If you can't find it, substitute your favorite cocoa mix.

Blueberry Pancakes from Hell

Here is a little recipe that combines two of my favorite tastes, sweet and hot. It was created in response to a challenge by my audio engineer, Mike Friese. For a few weeks Friese kept suggesting that I come up with a hot recipe for blueberries. Much to his surprise I prepared this during my Biker Breakfast Bonanza show. First you get the sweet taste, then the heat sneaks up—ALRIGHT!

> 1 fresh habanero pepper, stemmed, seeded, and minced
> 2 cups blueberries
> ½ cup honey
> 1 cup complete pancake mix, such as Bisquick
> ¾ cup water
> 2 tablespoons butter or margarine

Place the habanero, 1 cup of blueberries, and the honey in a food processor or a blender and puree the hell out of them. (If you want to do this by hand, use a medium mixing bowl and a potato masher. First pulverize the blueberries with the minced habanero, then use a wire whisk to whip in the honey. Don't spare the elbow grease—whip the daylights out of this stuff.)

To make the pancakes biker style, combine the pancake mix with the water as per package directions. When the mixture is well blended, grab a big fistful (or two) of the remaining blueberries, hold them over the bowl of pancake mix, and give them a big squeeze while hollering, "Alright!" Then mix them into the pancake mix.

Heat a griddle or frying pan and add the butter or margarine. Fry the pancakes until they are golden brown on both sides, about 4 minutes total. Serve piping hot with the blueberry syrup and a big glass of milk.

MAKES 6 TO 8 PANCAKES

Burning Baguettes

One Sunday, while waiting in the food line at a motorcycle club breakfast meeting, I had this devilish idea. You see, they were serving French toast that looked, well, a little burned. And then it happened—I started to daydream about the way to cook French toast Biker Billy–style. The result is this recipe, which will set your tongue on fire.

1 fresh habanero pepper, stemmed, seeded, and finely
     minced
4 large eggs
2 teaspoons chopped garlic
2 tablespoons half-and-half
1 tablespoon dried parsley
1 tablespoon paprika
Salt and ground black pepper
French bread slices
2 tablespoons butter or margarine, plus additional
     melted to serve
Warmed maple syrup or honey

In a food processor or blender, combine the minced habanero, eggs, garlic, half-and-half, parsley, and paprika and blend well. Add salt and black pepper to taste. (If you are doing this by hand, first beat the eggs with the habanero until well blended. Then add the garlic, half-and-half, parsley, and paprika and blend well. Add salt and black pepper to taste.)

Soak the bread slices in the egg mix.

Heat the 2 tablespoons butter or margarine in a skillet and fry the bread slices until golden brown on both sides, about 2 minutes per side. Serve piping hot with melted butter or margarine and syrup or honey.

MAKES ABOUT 8 SLICES

Salsafied Eggs

This is a truly twisted recipe. It's like building a motorcycle using the engine from a pickup truck. Imagine innocent little poached eggs—plain, bland, *dull* food. Now imagine those poor eggs in hell—that's right, drowning in a sea of hot salsa. Now the biker comes to the rescue and throws them a pepper ring for a life preserver. Just when the eggs think they are safe, the biker tosses them on a tortilla and smothers them with cheese, then thrusts them under a flaming broiler. Oh boy, let's eat!

    Olive oil
    Quick Salsa (page 45)
    1 yellow bell pepper, cored and cut into three ¾-inch
       rings
    1 red bell pepper, cored and cut into three ¾-inch
       rings
    6 jumbo eggs
    1 package (6-inch) corn or flour tortillas
    ½ cup shredded cheddar cheese
    ½ cup shredded Monterey jack cheese

Coat the bottom of a large sauté pan with olive oil and place over high heat. When the oil is hot, carefully pour the salsa into the sauté pan. You want about a ½- to ¾-inch-deep layer of salsa. The salsa must be very hot before you add the eggs.

Arrange the bell pepper rings in the hot salsa so that they are lying flat and level. One at a time, carefully break 1 egg into each bell pepper ring, being careful to keep the egg inside of the ring. Cover the pan and poach the eggs to desired firmness.

While the eggs are cooking, coat a heavy frying pan with olive oil. Fry 1 tortilla for each egg, until lightly browned on both sides. Keep warm.

continued

When the eggs are done, place 1 egg and its pepper ring on each tortilla. Spoon extra salsa around the edges to cover the tortilla. Dress with shredded cheese. Serve immediately.

MAKES 6 SALSAFIED EGGS

NOTE: If you wish to melt the cheese, place the eggs under the broiler for a minute, watching very carefully so the eggs don't overcook and the cheese doesn't burn.

Spanish Fire Omelet

Breakfast, lunch, or dinner, even as a midnight snack, this recipe is hot, easy, quick, and hits the spot when I get the urge. There is enough filling to make several omelets, which makes this a perfect recipe to prepare when you don't know how many hungry bikers are riding over for brunch.

3 tablespoons olive oil
1 fresh red jalapeño pepper, stemmed and minced
1 fresh green Anaheim pepper, stemmed and minced
1 fresh green serrano pepper, stemmed and minced
6 garlic cloves, minced
2 medium onions, minced
4 cups cooked rice
1 (28-ounce) can whole peeled tomatoes with juice,
    cut into large chunks
2 tablespoons margarine
6 large eggs, beaten

Heat the oil in a large frying pan over moderately high heat. Add the peppers, garlic, and onions. Stir well to coat and sauté until the onions are golden brown, 3 to 5 minutes.

Add the rice and stir well. Reduce the heat and simmer for 3 to 4 minutes, or until the rice begins to turn golden. Add the tomatoes and their juice, stir well, and cover. Simmer for 10 minutes, stirring occasionally to prevent burning. Remove from the heat.

Melt the margarine in a large frying pan over medium heat. Pour the eggs into the pan and fry, turning once. Cook until the eggs are firm and begin to brown at the edges, 3 to 5 minutes.

Cover half the eggs with a generous layer of the hot rice mixture. Fold the other half of the omelet over the rice, remove from frying pan, and serve immediately.

MAKES 6 TO 8 SERVINGS

Borderline Omelet

This recipe is on the edge of breakfast and brunch. It is a hearty meal that will fuel up the hungriest bikers in your club. In fact, just thinking about it gets me hungry for a plateful and makes me yearn for the road. Excuse me, but I have to answer the call of the wild sauté pan and the howling monster that wants out of my garage. Cook this while I'm gone and save me a serving or three. Alright!

There is enough filling to make several omelets, depending on how much bean mix you use. Extra filling is perfect for making burritos or tacos, or use it with Hot Flour Empanada Dough, page 226, or Hot Corn Empanada Dough, page 228, to make turnovers.

1 dried long slim cayenne pepper, stemmed and crushed
1 ancho pepper, stemmed and torn into small pieces
½ cup boiling water (see page 18)
Peanut oil
1 to 2 medium onions, diced
1 yellow bell pepper, cored and cut into 1-inch squares
1 green bell pepper, cored and cut into 1-inch squares
1 (16-ounce) can pink beans, rinsed and drained
1 large tomato, diced
2 to 3 teaspoons chopped garlic
½ teaspoon turmeric
½ teaspoon ground cumin
1 teaspoon ground black pepper
1 teaspoon salt
2 tablespoons margarine
6 jumbo eggs, beaten
½ cup shredded cheddar cheese

Place the cayenne and ancho peppers in small bowl, cover with the boiling water, and set aside. Allow to cool to room temperature.

Heat several tablespoons of the oil in a large frying pan over medium heat. Add the onions and bell peppers and fry for 1 minute. Add the re-

hydrated hot peppers with their soaking water and stir well. Stir in the pink beans and simmer for about 3 minutes, or until the onions are transparent. Stir in the tomato, garlic, and seasonings, reduce the heat to low, and simmer until the tomatoes cook down into a sauce, 10 to 15 minutes. Remove from the heat.

Melt the margarine in a medium skillet. Add the beaten eggs. Cook, turning once, until firm. Cover half the eggs with a generous layer of the bean filling, add a generous layer of cheese, and carefully fold the uncovered half of the eggs over the cheese and beans. Cook briefly until the cheese melts, about 1 minute. Remove from the frying pan and serve immediately.

MAKES 4 TO 6 SERVINGS

Hot Hash Browns

Serving breakfast eggs without potatoes is like going riding without the proper riding gear—you just shouldn't. With this recipe you'll never have to.

3 tablespoons margarine, or more as needed
1 fresh red jalapeño pepper, stemmed and minced
1 medium onion, diced
4 teaspoons chopped garlic
2 medium potatoes, unpeeled, cut into ¼-inch cubes
Liquid Smoke
Salt and ground black pepper

In a large frying pan, melt the margarine over high heat. Add the jalapeño pepper, onion, garlic, and potatoes. Stir well and sprinkle with several dashes of Liquid Smoke.

Reduce the heat to medium and sauté the potatoes, turning often, for 7 to 10 minutes, or until they are golden brown and tender. You may have to add more margarine to keep them from sticking to the pan. Add salt and pepper to taste. Serve piping hot.

MAKES 2 TO 4 SERVINGS

Biker-Style Cheese Grits

I love Southern food, especially the Southern breakfast staple grits, which is always available in the South but almost never in the North. I will ride a few hundred miles before breakfast just to be at a truck stop that serves grits. Try them; you may find your motorcycle tends to head south in the morning.

2 tablespoons margarine

1 fresh red jalapeño pepper, stemmed and minced

1 medium yellow onion, diced

2 cups water

2 teaspoons chopped garlic

⅛ teaspoon ground cumin

Salt and ground black pepper

½ cup quick grits

1 cup shredded cheddar cheese

In a 1-quart saucepan, melt the margarine. Add the jalapeño pepper and onion, reduce the heat, and simmer 2 to 3 minutes, or until the onion is tender but not brown. Add the water and increase the heat to high. Stir in the garlic, cumin, and salt and black pepper to taste. When the water comes to a rolling boil, slowly add the quick grits, stirring constantly. Boil and stir for 1 minute. Reduce the heat to very low, cover, and cook for 5 to 7 minutes, stirring occasionally. Stir in the cheddar cheese and serve immediately.

MAKES ABOUT 4 SERVINGS

NOTE: If you like a thinner or smoother texture, add more water and cook a little longer. Put leftover grits in a greased loaf pan and refrigerate. Cut the leftover grits into slices and fry them in a little margarine for tomorrow's breakfast.

Hot Apple-Mango-Raisin Compote

If you love pancakes, waffles, or toast but your tongue says "Hey, give me some fire!" just add this to your breakfast table and toss that dull jelly over your shoulder. (Remember to look over your shoulder first; you want to make sure the garbage can is where it should be.)

> 1 (15-ounce) can sliced mangoes in syrup, cut into large chunks
> 2 golden delicious apples, cored, peeled, and cut into large chunks
> ½ cup golden raisins
> ½ fresh habanero pepper, stemmed and seeded
> ⅓ cup honey

In a small saucepan, heat the mangoes and syrup over medium heat. Add the apples, raisins, and pepper and bring to a boil. Reduce the heat to low and simmer for 10 minutes.

Drain the fruit, reserving the liquid, and set aside. Return the liquid to the pot, along with the habanero, add the honey, and bring the mixture to a boil. Reduce the heat to low and simmer for 5 minutes.

Remove the habanero and discard. Return the fruit to the pot, stir well to coat with the syrup, and reheat for 1 minute. Serve warm.

MAKES ABOUT 2 CUPS

Lunch and Other
Handy Foods

ONE OF my favorite ways to lunch is at a roadside rest where I can pull out my brown bag and watch the eagles soar. Whether you're picnicking solo or with friends, or spending an afternoon in the garage restoring a classic motorcycle, lunch should be robust and have lots of flavor and fire. Wimpy sandwiches just won't cut it. The recipes in this chapter will calm the lunch-crazed bikers in your garage, and they are hearty enough to serve at dinner. So let's do lunch biker-style.

Black Bean Burritos

Classic riding clothes are made of black leather, and nothing comes close to the feeling of riding in well-worn leather. Well, when I cook a classic bean burrito, what kind of beans do you think I use? Black beans. Other beans will do in a pinch, but black beans have that certain edge that this hothead biker desires.

¼ cup olive oil

7 garlic cloves, thinly sliced

4 medium onions, thinly sliced

2 fresh jalapeño peppers, stemmed and thinly sliced

1 (16-ounce) can black beans

5 plum tomatoes, peeled

1 cup water

Liquid Smoke

Salt and ground black pepper

Six to eight 10-inch flour tortillas (see Note, page 85)

TO ASSEMBLE:

Shredded lettuce

Diced tomato

Diced onion

Broccoli florets

1 cup shredded cheddar cheese

Quick Salsa (optional; page 45)

Sour cream (optional)

Heat the oil in a large frying pan over medium heat. Add the garlic, onions, and jalapeño peppers and fry for 3 to 4 minutes, or until the onions begin to brown. Add the beans with their liquid and simmer until the mixture begins to stick to the bottom of the pan.

Add the tomatoes, cutting them into chunks right in the frying pan.

Add the water and several dashes of Liquid Smoke and stir well. Simmer for 2 to 4 minutes, or until the mixture thickens. Remove half the mixture from the pan and use a fork or potato masher to turn the beans into a paste. Add the salt and black pepper to taste, stir thoroughly, and return to the pan.

Put a tortilla on a plate. Place several tablespoons of the bean mixture on the lower third of the tortilla, forming a line from the left edge extending to 2 inches from the right edge. Cover with vegetables of your choice and a generous layer of cheese, then add some of the salsa and/or sour cream. Fold the near end of the tortilla over the filling. Then fold the right end over the filling (this creates the bottom of the burrito), and roll up the burrito away from you. Repeat with the remaining tortillas. Serve hot with extra salsa on the side.

MAKES 6 TO 8 BURRITOS

Hot Garbanzo Bean Patties

My sense of taste is most satisfied by a balanced blend of complex spices, fire, and contrasting textures. Throw in a rich aroma, and look out. This recipe has all those things in a handy sandwich. And best of all, it is always available at a special place that has the best table reserved just for you: home. Take your taste buds for a ride with this recipe.

1 or more dried **New Mexico** peppers, stemmed and torn into small pieces

5 garlic cloves, minced

1 small onion, minced

1 (16-ounce) can garbanzo beans, drained, liquid reserved

²⁄₃ cup crushed corn chips, medium coarse

¼ teaspoon dried cumin

¼ teaspoon dried basil

¼ teaspoon dried marjoram

¼ teaspoon ground black pepper

¾ teaspoon salt

½ teaspoon turmeric

2 tablespoons dried parsley

½ teaspoon baking soda

1 tablespoon yellow cornmeal, plus extra for breading

1 tablespoon tahini (see Note, page 52)

1 jumbo egg, lightly beaten

Oil, for frying

TO ASSEMBLE:

Pita bread
Shredded lettuce
Diced onion
Diced red bell pepper
Diced tomatoes
Tahini Sauce (page 66)

In small saucepan, combine the New Mexico pepper, garlic, onion, and ½ cup liquid from the garbanzo beans. Heat on low until the mixture starts to boil. Remove from the heat and set aside to cool.

In a large mixing bowl, crush the garbanzo beans with a fork or potato masher. You want a chunky mixture, not a puree. Add the crushed corn chips and stir to combine. Add the seasonings, baking soda, 1 tablespoon cornmeal, and tahini and stir to combine. Add the pepper mixture and stir to combine. Stir in the egg, cover, and refrigerate for 30 to 60 minutes to firm up the mixture and let the flavors blend. In the meantime, prepare the condiments.

Heat several inches of oil in a deep pot or deep-fryer to 365°F.

Form the garbanzo mixture into 1- to 1½-inch balls, roll them in cornmeal, flatten, and fry in hot oil until golden brown or darker, 2 to 4 minutes. Drain on paper towels.

Place 3 or 4 patties in a pita pocket, add a handful of vegetables, spoon on some tahini sauce, and enjoy.

MAKES ABOUT 18 PATTIES

Heart-Y Biker Tacos

Tacos are a perfect biker food—they can be customized to satisfy your taste. This recipe has some performance modifications; after all, why customize if you don't add some muscle to the stock motor? The "motor" of a taco is usually beef or pork, but that's where I've made changes for more taste and less fat and cholesterol. Midland Harvest's Taco Filling 'n Dip mix is a product of American agriculture and ingenuity. ALRIGHT, Archer Daniels Midland (ADM). Of course, you can always use 16 ounces of quality ground meat instead—just reduce the cold water to ½ cup and adjust the cooking time.

> 1 ancho pepper, stemmed and torn into small pieces
> ¼ cup boiling water (see page 18)
> Peanut oil
> 1 medium onion, coarsely chopped
> 5 garlic cloves, coarsely chopped
> ½ red bell pepper, cored and diced
> 2 plum tomatoes, chopped
> 1 (6-ounce) package Midland Harvest Taco Filling 'n Dip
>   mix (see Note)
> 1½ cups cold water
> 8 to 12 taco shells

TO ASSEMBLE:

> Shredded lettuce
> Diced tomatoes
> Chopped onion
> Shredded cheddar cheese
> Ancho Pepper Sauce (optional; page 60)

Place the ancho pepper in a small bowl and cover with boiling water. Allow to cool to room temperature, then puree the mixture in a

blender or food processor equipped with a chopping blade. Set aside.

Cover the bottom of a large frying pan with peanut oil and place over medium heat. Add the onion and garlic and fry for 3 to 5 minutes or until the onion is golden brown. Stir in the ancho puree. Add the bell pepper and fry for 2 to 4 minutes or until the pepper is tender. Add the tomatoes with their juice and stir to combine.

Add the taco filling mix and water and stir well to moisten the mix. Bring the mixture to a boil and then lower the heat and simmer for 10 to 12 minutes.

Warm the taco shells according to package directions. Place a few spoonfuls of taco filling into each shell. Add a handful of shredded lettuce, diced tomatoes, chopped onion, and shredded cheese. Top with Ancho Pepper Sauce, or just serve the tacos with the sauce on the side.

MAKES 8 TO 12 TACOS

NOTE: The Midland Harvest Taco Filling 'n Dip mix (and the Burger 'n Loaf mix in the recipe on page 93) uses TVP (texturized vegetable protein) as a replacement for meat. TVP is usually based on soybean proteins, contains no cholesterol, and is low-fat. The texture is excellent, making this a good replacement for meat if you are trying to reduce the cholesterol in your diet. You can substitute another brand of soy protein taco mix that produces 16 ounces of finished product, although you may have to adjust the cold water and cooking time according to the package directions.

French Bread Pizza from Hell

Why is it that this pizza, made on Italian bread, is called a French bread pizza? Who cares! Enjoy it on Italian or any other kind of bread.

Olive oil

2 fresh red jalapeño peppers, stemmed and thinly sliced

1 red bell pepper, cored and julienned

1 yellow bell pepper, cored and julienned

1 orange bell pepper, cored and julienned

1 green bell pepper, cored and julienned

1 Italian green frying pepper, cored and julienned

3 medium onions, julienned

5 teaspoons chopped garlic

Salt and ground black pepper

1 loaf Italian bread

2 cups shredded mozzarella, or to taste

Heat several tablespoons of olive oil in a large frying pan over medium heat. Add the jalapeños, bell peppers, Italian frying pepper, onions, and garlic and fry for 6 to 10 minutes, or until the peppers are tender. Add salt and black pepper to taste.

Preheat the oven to 350°F.

Cut the Italian bread in half lengthwise. Cover with a generous amount of shredded mozzarella, add a layer of sautéed peppers and some oil from the frying pan, and top with a light layer of cheese. Bake until the cheese is melted, 10 to 12 minutes. Serve hot.

MAKES 6 TO 8 SERVINGS

Biker Burgers

Burgers are as American as apple pie and the flag, but these days they are nearly as politically incorrect as bikers. What's going on? Well, bikers get a bad rap because some people think the way we travel is too dangerous (read fun). Burgers are considered at least as dangerous because of the cholesterol they contain. Only you can help make bikers safe on the roadways, but this recipe can help make your burgers safer! These burgers are meat free; you'll be pleasantly surprised how delicious they taste, and the texture will blow you away. This recipe uses Midland Harvest's Burger 'n Loaf mix (see Note, page 91). If you prefer, you can substitute 16 ounces of quality ground meat, reduce the boiling water to ½ cup, omit the cool water, and adjust the cooking time. Either way, Eat Hot, Ride Safe, and wave the flag because bikers and burgers are here to stay!

3 sun-dried tomatoes, thinly sliced

3 teaspoons chopped garlic

1 tablespoon paprika

1 ancho pepper, stemmed and torn into small pieces

1 dried long slim cayenne pepper, stemmed and crushed

1 cup boiling water (see page 18)

1 (6-ounce) package Midland Harvest Burger 'n Loaf mix

6 tablespoons cool water

Place the sun-dried tomatoes, garlic, paprika, and ancho and cayenne peppers in a small bowl and cover with boiling water. Allow to cool to room temperature, then puree the mixture in a blender or food processor equipped with a chopping blade. Scrape the mixture into a 1-cup measure, adding cool water as needed until it equals 1 full cup.

Place the Burger 'n Loaf mix in a medium mixing bowl. Add the pureed mixture and the 6 tablespoons water. Mix thoroughly and let stand for 15 minutes.

continued

Form the mixture into patties or "meat" balls and barbecue or fry as you would hamburgers, allowing 2 to 3 minutes a side, or until they reach the desired crispness. Serve piping hot.

MAKES 4 BURGERS

Sloppy Bikers

If this recipe title sounds like a redundancy, then you haven't met some of my riding buddies. You would be amazed at how clean and shiny they keep their bikes and riding gear. So you ask why this recipe is called "Sloppy Bikers"? In part it's named for my on-camera cooking style, but it is also a warning—these saucy "burgers" can get sloppy if the kaiser rolls are overloaded. But the taste is worth the risk. I have used Midland Harvest Taco Filling 'n Dip mix (see Note, page 91) to provide a heart-healthy version of the classic sloppy Joe, and of course I have imbued them with my fiery style. You can substitute 1 pound of high-quality ground meat. Reduce the water by 1 cup, cook the meat until it is well done, and season it with salt and ground black pepper. Try these burgers both ways. Just be sure to keep your bike clean!

  1 ancho pepper, stemmed and torn into small pieces
  2 dried long slim cayenne peppers, stemmed and crushed
  1½ cups boiling water (see page 18)
  2 tablespoons margarine
  1 medium red onion, coarsely chopped
  2 plum tomatoes, diced
  2 teaspoons chopped garlic
  1 (6-ounce) package Midland Harvest Taco Filling 'n
    Dip mix
  4 to 5 kaiser rolls, sliced in half crosswise

Place the ancho and cayenne peppers in a small bowl and cover with boiling water. Set side and allow to cool to room temperature.

In a large frying pan, melt the margarine over medium heat. Add the onion and tomatoes and sauté for 3 to 5 minutes, or until the onions are golden brown.

Combine the peppers and water, sautéed onion mixture, and garlic in a food processor fitted with a chopping blade. Pulse a few times to chop

well, but do not puree. Transfer the chopped mixture to the frying pan and add the taco filling mix. Stir well to moisten and simmer over low heat for 10 to 12 minutes.

Place a generous scoop of the mixture on each roll and serve immediately.

MAKES 4 TO 5 SLOPPY BIKERS

Biker Beerritos*

I love bean burritos. In fact, I can cook them six ways from Sunday and never make the same thing twice. This recipe came about in response to a Viewer Recipe Contest entry that suggested using beer—hence "beer-ritos." Alright, Eric and Heidi Schnell, these Biker Beerritos are for you. And thanks for another excuse to cook with fire.

    2 tablespoons extra-virgin olive oil
    2 tablespoons chopped garlic
    2 medium onions, diced
    2 fresh cherry peppers, minced
    1 (19-ounce) can large red kidney beans, drained
    1 tablespoon Liquid Smoke
    ½ teaspoon ground black pepper
    ½ teaspoon salt
    ½ teaspoon ground cumin
    1 yellow bell pepper, cored and julienned
    1 ripe beefsteak tomato, pureed
    1 tablespoon dark molasses
    1 (12-ounce) bottle beer, preferably dark beer
    Eight to ten 10-inch flour tortillas (see Note, page 85)
    1 cup shredded cheddar cheese, or to taste
    Quick Salsa (optional; page 45)
    Sour cream (optional)

Heat the olive oil in a large sauté pan over high heat. Add the garlic, onions, and cherry peppers, stir to coat with oil, and sauté for 3 to 5 minutes, or until the onions are golden brown. Add the beans, Liquid Smoke, black pepper, salt, and cumin. Reduce the heat to medium, stir well, and simmer for about 10 minutes or until the liquid is absorbed.

Add the bell pepper and tomato puree, stir well, and simmer for 8 to 10 minutes, or until the liquid is absorbed. Reduce the heat to low, add the molasses and the beer, and simmer for 8 to 10 minutes, or until the sauce is reduced to a thick and creamy consistency.

continued

Put a tortilla on a plate. Place several tablespoons of the filling on the lower third of the tortilla, forming a line from the left edge extending to 2 inches from the right edge. Cover with a generous layer of cheese, then add some of the salsa and/or sour cream. Fold the near end of the tortilla over the filling. Then fold the right end over the filling (this creates the bottom of the burrito) and roll up the burrito away from you. Repeat with the remaining tortillas. Serve hot with extra salsa on the side.

MAKES 8 TO 10 BURRITOS

Contest winner

Three Bean Tacos

This taco recipe is a Mexican biker–style bean extravaganza. The medley of the three beans in concert with the ancho pepper and scallions is music to my taste buds. Although the fire level is only medium, the taste level is maximum. One taco is all it will take to get your bike headed for the border. Cook them and enjoy the flavor fiesta!

1 ancho pepper, stemmed and seeded
¼ cup boiling water (see page 18)
2 tablespoons peanut oil
1 carrot, peeled and cut into ¼-inch slices
6 scallions
1 cup canned pinto beans, rinsed
1 cup canned small red beans, rinsed
1 cup canned black beans, rinsed
½ teaspoon ground cumin
½ teaspoon ground black pepper
½ teaspoon salt
½ teaspoon hot Hungarian paprika
½ teaspoon dried oregano
1 cup Quick Salsa (page 45)
10 to 12 taco shells

TO ASSEMBLE:

Shredded lettuce
Diced tomato
Shredded cheddar cheese
Ancho Pepper Sauce (optional; page 60)

Place the pepper in a small bowl and cover with boiling water. Set aside to cool to room temperature.

Heat the oil in a large sauté pan over medium heat. Add the carrot,

stir well to coat, and sauté for 2 to 3 minutes. While the carrot is sautéing, trim the scallions. Remove the dark green tops and set aside; cut the white and light green sections into ½-inch-thick slices. Add the sliced scallions to the sauté pan, reduce the heat to low, and sauté for 2 to 3 minutes, or until the carrot starts to brown.

Add the beans, stir well, and sauté for 5 to 8 minutes, or until the beans begin to stick to the bottom of the pan.

Puree the rehydrated ancho pepper and the cumin, black pepper, salt, paprika, and oregano in a blender for 30 seconds, or until the mixture is smooth and free of large pieces. Add the puree and the salsa to the sauté pan and simmer for 5 to 8 minutes, or until the sauce is very thick. As the sauce simmers, thinly slice the dark green scallion tops.

Warm the taco shells according to package directions.

Place a few spoonfuls of the filling into the taco shells. Add some shredded lettuce, diced tomato, scallion greens, and shredded cheddar cheese. Serve with Ancho Pepper Sauce on the side.

MAKES 10 TO 12 TACOS

Soups

WINTER riding has its own special pleasures and rhythms. The cold air is so crisp and clear, it turns your breath into a fog on your face shield. When you stop, the warmth rising off your rumbling motor will barely thaw your gloved hands. While you roll down the road knowing that warmth awaits at the ride's end, you must watch your speed or the wind will make you colder. Bewildered motorists look at you in amazement: the sight of you makes them feel freezing in their cars, and they wonder how you can ride in the cold. Ah, freedom—the cold air washes over you, cleansing the cabin fever from your soul. From deep inside your shell of frozen black leather you repeat the mantra that will get you home to hot and nourishing soup. The mantra sounds in rhythm with the big motor: thump, thump, soup, soup. At last you're happily home, and the fire crackles to warm your toes. The ride has made your soul feel light and free; now the soup warms your body from within as you begin to think of the next ride, then of spring.

Soup is the symbol of warmth and home in the midst of winter. But even if you're not a four-season rider, you'll enjoy the soups in this chapter! They are doubly warming from the heat and a little extra fire.

Hot Potato Corn Chowder

Every so often at a poker run I'll spot a simple, classic bike. Uncluttered by added chrome and accessories, it's almost like sculpture. I also enjoy foods that have a straightforward, down-home taste. Nothing fancy, just food that makes me feel comfortable and secure. This soup always gives me that feeling. After a big steaming bowl, you will feel that all is right with the world.

> 4 cups parboiled potatoes, peeled, or 2 (16-ounce) cans
>   whole peeled potatoes, drained
> 3 tablespoons salted butter
> 2 fresh long slim red cayenne peppers, stemmed
> 1 medium onion, coarsely chopped
> 1 (12-ounce) can whole kernel corn, drained
> 1 cup water
> 2 cups whole milk or half-and-half
> ½ teaspoon salt
> 1 teaspoon ground black pepper

Cut the potatoes into ¾-inch chunks and set aside.

In a large soup pot, melt the butter over low heat. Add the whole peppers and sauté for 1 to 2 minutes. Add the onion and the potatoes, stir well to coat with butter, increase the heat to medium, and sauté until the onions turn golden brown, 5 to 8 minutes.

Mash the potatoes into smaller, bite-sized chunks. Add the corn, water, milk, salt, and black pepper. Stir well and reduce the heat to low. Cover and simmer for 1 hour, stirring often to keep the corn from sticking to the bottom of the pot. Remove the cayenne peppers before serving.

MAKES ABOUT 4 SERVINGS

Nuclear Nutty Soup

The combination of peanut butter, cashews, and coconut in this soup is unbelievable, but fantastic. Add the power of a habanero pepper and it is totally atomic. Like stuffing two Harley engines into one frame and feeding them nitro-laced fuel, you get the green light, crack the throttle WFO, and count the seconds to eternity. Go drag racing with your taste buds—cook this soup and chase the sky.

> 1 dried habanero pepper, stemmed and seeded
> ¼ cup boiling water (see page 18)
> 4 tablespoons (½ stick) salted butter
> 1 medium onion, halved and thinly sliced
> 1 celery stalk, thinly sliced crosswise
> 1 cup cashew pieces, coarsely chopped
> 1 cup sweetened shredded coconut
> 1 cup chunky peanut butter
> 1 cup half-and-half or light cream
> 2 cups hot water

Soak the habanero pepper in the boiling water for 5 minutes. Puree the habanero and the soaking water in a blender or a food processor equipped with a chopping blade and set aside to cool.

In a large saucepan, melt the butter over low heat. Add the onion and celery and sauté, stirring often, for 2 to 3 minutes, or until the onion is transparent. Add the cashews, coconut, and pureed habanero and stir well.

Whisk the peanut butter into the saucepan a few tablespoons at a time. Each addition of peanut butter should melt before adding the next measure. When all the peanut butter is melted, add the half-and-half slowly while whisking continuously. While still whisking, slowly add the hot water. Reduce the heat to the lowest possible, cover, and simmer for 1 hour, stirring the soup often to prevent burning and separation. Do *not* allow it to boil.

Transfer a cup of soup at a time to a blender or a food processor

equipped with a chopping blade. Pulse several times and transfer to a soup tureen. Serve hot, ladling out portions to distribute the nuts and coconut. (This soup can be kept warm in the top of a double boiler over hot, not boiling, water.)

MAKES ABOUT 6 SERVINGS

Black-Eyed Soup

When I was a child, I loved visiting relatives in the South because of all the different foods we ate while there. Many of the dishes I most enjoyed were looked down on as "poor folk's food" in the North. One such food is black-eyed peas, and I especially enjoy them in this stick-to-your-ribs soup.

3 tablespoons salted butter

2 medium onions, minced

1 fresh long slim red cayenne pepper, minced

1 (15-ounce) can black-eyed peas, rinsed

2 carrots, peeled and cut into ¼-inch slices

½ teaspoon salt

¼ teaspoon black pepper

1 teaspoon dried parsley

⅛ teaspoon celery seeds

1½ cups cool water

⅛ teaspoon ground cumin

In a cast-iron skillet, melt 2 tablespoons of butter over medium heat. Add the onions and cayenne pepper and sauté 3 to 5 minutes, or until the onions are golden brown.

Place the black-eyed peas, carrots, salt, black pepper, parsley, and celery seeds in a 2-quart saucepan and cover with water. Bring to a boil. Add the sautéed onions and cayenne pepper, reduce the heat to low, and simmer for 30 to 45 minutes. Stir often to prevent the peas from sticking to the bottom of the pot. Remove the soup from the heat and allow to cool. Puree in a food processor or blender with the remaining 1 tablespoon of butter and the cumin. Return to the saucepan, reheat, and serve. (This soup is very thick. If you would like a thinner consistency just add a little water while you puree it. It may tend to separate, and if so, stir well before serving.)

MAKES 4 TO 6 SERVINGS

Mean Black Bean Soup

This is a powerful soup, not intended for the faint of heart. If you like point-and-shoot firepower that will smoke the competition, this soup is for you. Strap on your helmet and hold on to your spoon—this is the bad boy of the soup world.

If desired, serve this with some Cornmeal Dumplings (page 230) and sour cream or shredded cheddar cheese.

> 1 ancho pepper, stemmed, seeded, and torn into small
>   pieces
> 1 dried long slim cayenne pepper, stemmed and crushed
> ¼ cup boiling water (see page 18)
> 2 tablespoons extra-virgin olive oil
> 1 medium onion, minced
> 1 carrot, peeled and minced
> 1 celery stalk, minced
> ½ cup peeled whole tomatoes with their juice
> ½ teaspoon black pepper
> ¼ teaspoon dried oregano
> 1 teaspoon salt
> ¼ teaspoon ground cumin
> 1 (19-ounce) can black beans
> 1 (12-ounce) bottle stout or dark beer

Place the ancho and cayenne peppers in a small bowl. Cover with boiling water and set aside to cool.

Heat the oil in a large soup pot over medium heat. Add the onion, carrot, and celery, stir well to coat with oil, and sauté for 2 to 3 minutes, or until the onion is transparent.

While the onion is sautéing, puree the rehydrated peppers along with the tomatoes in a blender for 1 minute, until smooth and free of chunks. Add the puree and the remaining ingredients to the pot. Bring the soup to a boil, then reduce the heat to low. Cover and simmer for 30 min-

utes, stirring often to prevent the beans from sticking to the bottom of the pot.

Using a slotted spoon, remove 1 cup of the beans and set aside. Puree the rest of the soup in the blender or a food processor. Return the puree and the reserved beans to the pot and reheat over the lowest possible heat. Stir well before serving.

MAKES 4 TO 6 SERVINGS

NOTE: If you find that the soup is a little sharp tasting from the beer, stir in a tablespoon or two of molasses to take the "meanness" out.

Triple-Shot Hot Stock

Soup stock may seem mysterious, like desmo valve gear on a Ducati motorcycle. But fear not, you don't need a degree in advanced Italian engineering to produce a high-performance soup stock. Follow this recipe and your soups will always have extra horsepower without unnecessary cholesterol.

    6 quarts water
    3 dried New Mexico peppers, stemmed
    3 ancho peppers, stemmed
    3 dried long slim cayenne peppers, stemmed
    6 medium onions
    3 carrots
    1 head of garlic, separated into cloves and peeled
       (about 24 cloves)

Combine all the ingredients in a large stockpot and bring to a boil over high heat. Reduce the heat to low and simmer, covered, for 2 hours, stirring every 10 minutes.

Strain the stock and discard the solid material (see Note). This should yield 5 quarts of clear stock. If less, add water to make 5 quarts before using or dividing for storage; this will ensure proper results when used in recipes in this book.

MAKES 5 QUARTS

NOTE: You can create a thick stock from this recipe. Prepare as above but puree the solid ingredients after cooking. Combine the puree with the stock and stir well. Strain the mixture to remove pepper seeds and skins, then stir well before dividing for use or storage.

Not Gentle Lentil Soup

This recipe offers all the comfort of lentil soup, but it is loaded with high-performance taste. It will give your taste buds a real thrill.

2 cups dried lentils, picked clean and rinsed

10 cups clear Triple-Shot Hot Stock (page 110)

3 tablespoons salted butter

1 medium onion, coarsely chopped

4 garlic cloves, minced

1 chipotle pepper packed in adobo sauce, minced

1 teaspoon ground black pepper

1 teaspoon salt

½ teaspoon ground cumin

3 tablespoons flour

1 cup cool water

Combine the lentils and stock in a large soup pot. Bring to a boil over high heat. Reduce the heat to low and simmer for 2 to 4 hours or until the lentils are tender.

Use a slotted spoon to remove 1 cup of the lentils. Puree the lentils with 1 cup of the broth in a blender for 1 minute until smooth. Return the puree to the soup, stir well, and continue to simmer.

While the soup is simmering, melt the butter in a small sauté pan over medium heat. Sauté the onion, garlic, chipotle pepper, black pepper, salt, and cumin for 3 to 5 minutes, or until the onion is golden brown. Slowly stir in the flour and sauté for about 5 minutes while constantly stirring until the flour turns a golden brown.

Remove the sauté pan from the heat and slowly add the cool water while stirring. Stir with a wire whisk until the mixture is smooth and the pan is cleaned. Pour this mixture into the soup while stirring. Simmer for 30 minutes to 1 hour more over very low heat, stirring often. Adjust seasoning with salt and black pepper to taste before serving.

MAKES 6 TO 8 SERVINGS

Mulligatawny My Way

This classic Indian-style soup (whose name means "pepper water") is fantastic. I've changed the type of pepper, replaced the *ghee* (clarified butter) with margarine, and adjusted the spices to suit my taste buds. Try it my way first before customizing it to your own specifications.

> 2 tablespoons margarine
> 2 dried New Mexico peppers, stemmed, seeded, and crushed
> 1 teaspoon cumin seeds
> 1 teaspoon whole black peppercorns
> ½ cup boiling water (see page 18)
> 2 medium onions, coarsely chopped
> 4 cups cool water
> 1½ cups dried pink or yellow lentils, picked clean and rinsed (see Note)
> 1 teaspoon turmeric
> 1 cardamom pod
> 1 teaspoon salt

In a small sauté pan, melt the margarine over medium heat. Add the New Mexico peppers, cumin seeds, and peppercorns to the sauté pan. Sauté for about 2 minutes or until the margarine is a rich brown color.

Use a slotted spoon to transfer the New Mexico peppers, cumin seeds, and peppercorns to a small heatproof bowl, leaving as much margarine as possible in the pan. Cover the peppers, cumin seeds, and peppercorns with the boiling water and let stand for about 10 minutes.

Return the sauté pan to medium heat and add the onions. Sauté for 2 to 3 minutes, or until the onions are transparent. Remove from the heat. In a blender or food processor equipped with a chopping blade, puree the rehydrated New Mexico peppers, cumin seeds, peppercorns, and sautéed onions for 1 minute until smooth. If necessary add a little of the cool water to help produce a smooth puree.

In a medium soup pot, combine the lentils, remaining cool water,

turmeric, cardamom pod, and salt. Place the soup pot over medium heat and bring to a boil. Add the puree, reduce the heat to low, and simmer, covered, for 20 to 25 minutes or until the lentils are tender. (If you are using yellow lentils, increase the simmering time to 40 to 45 minutes.)

Transfer the soup to a blender or food processor equipped with a chopping blade and puree for 30 seconds to 1 minute until smooth. (Before pureeing you can remove the whole cardamom pod if you want less cardamom flavor; I leave it in.) The soup can be passed through a fine strainer if you want to remove any small pieces of pepper or lentil skin; I don't because this reduces the dietary fiber content. Serve warm.

MAKES 4 TO 6 SERVINGS

NOTE: Both pink and yellow lentils are staples in Indian cooking and can be obtained in Indian grocery stores and many health food stores. Sometime you'll find red lentils—these are just pink lentils traveling incognito. Whether pink (red) or yellow, they are split in half, unlike the Western brown lentils commonly used to make lentil soup. If you can't find the Indian lentils, don't substitute brown lentils; yellow split peas would be a better choice.

Pasta and More

I AM always amazed at the wonders that can be produced from flour and water. Add a little oil, salt, and maybe some eggs—ALRIGHT, it's pasta. From extra-thin vermicelli to the richest stuffed shells, there is something for everyone. You could say that pasta is the V-twin engine of the food world. Compare America's Harley V-twin and Italy's Ducati V-twin; the two engines are similar but also very different. Even the multiple ways they function can be compared. Harley, Moto Guzzi, and Ducati all use V-twins, but each differently. Pasta can be everything from the foundation that wears a sauce, to the wrapper for a filling, to just another ingredient in a casserole.

Pasta's role as a foundation for a sauce is probably its most common, and several of the recipes here demonstrate just how different pastas and sauces can be. There is one tomato-based sauce, and several of the stuffed pastas have a sauce recipe that you can also use over pasta. You can also try the "sauce" from French Bread Pizza from Hell (page 92). Where a recipe calls for a particular shape of pasta, I have listed my preference, but you can substitute an equal amount of another shape. The recipes don't specify salting the water for cooking pasta. It can be salted

to taste, or, if you are on a low-salt diet, omit the salt. Try making the fresh pasta recipes. It is much easier to create homemade pasta than you might think. A fancy machine is not a prerequisite to successful pasta making, but a large flat surface for rolling the dough is helpful.

Zesty Fresh Pasta Sauce

Like a radical custom chopper, this recipe breaks away from tradition to find a new, more exciting personal expression. The whole idea is to create a fresh-from-the-garden taste and texture that will remind you of summer rides through farmlands and snack stops at farm stands. Make your favorite fresh pasta dish and serve it with this sauce, but be prepared—it is so fast and easy that you may never buy a jar of "sauce" again.

3 broccoli stalks

Olive oil

2 small zucchini, halved lengthwise and cut into ¼-inch slices

1½ to 2 dried New Mexico peppers, stemmed and crushed

7 garlic cloves, thinly sliced

2 medium onions, coarsely chopped

1 red bell pepper, cored and cut into ½-inch pieces

1 green bell pepper, cored and cut into ½-inch pieces

1¼ pounds fresh plum tomatoes, peeled and coarsely chopped, or 1 (28-ounce) can peeled whole plum tomatoes, coarsely chopped, with their juice

Remove the broccoli florets from the stalks. Break or cut the florets into bite-size pieces and set aside. Trim any leaves or hard dry parts from the broccoli stalks. Cut the stalks into ¼-inch slices.

Cover the bottom of a large sauté pan with olive oil and place over medium heat. Add the broccoli slices and zucchini and stir to coat with oil. Sauté for 2 to 3 minutes, or until the zucchini is tender. Add the New Mexico peppers, garlic, onions, and bell peppers and stir well to coat with oil. Sauté for 3 to 5 minutes, or until the onions begin to brown.

continued

Add the plum tomatoes and stir well. Bring to a boil, reduce the heat, and simmer, stirring often, until the tomatoes begin to break down. Add the broccoli florets and continue to simmer 5 to 10 minutes, or until the florets turn dark and the sauce thickens. Serve immediately over your favorite pasta.

MAKES 6 TO 8 CUPS

Lucifer's Angel Pasta

Some people see bikers as bad guys and gals on the Devil's own business; others know us as good Samaritans who donate time and money to charity. On weekends, dressed in black leather to protect ourselves from the elements and the possibility of a surprise encounter with the road surface, we look bad to some people. Those same people can meet us Monday through Friday and see a police officer, doctor, mechanic, or judge —just another person like themselves. Devil or angel, what we are all depends on who is judging us. Give a biker a chance, and you might just meet your best friend. Then invite that best friend over for some Lucifer's Angel Pasta; together you can judge if this recipe is devilish or angelic.

> 14 sun-dried tomatoes, thinly sliced
>
> 7 teaspoons chopped garlic
>
> 2 dried long slim cayenne peppers, stemmed and crushed
>
> 1 ancho pepper, stemmed, seeded, and torn into small
>   pieces
>
> 1 cup boiling water (see page 18)
>
> 12 scallions
>
> ½ cup olive oil
>
> 1 pound angel hair pasta

Fill a large pot with water and bring to a boil to cook the pasta.

Combine the sun-dried tomatoes, garlic, and cayenne and ancho peppers in a small bowl and cover with the boiling water. Set aside and allow to cool to room temperature.

Trim the scallions. Remove the dark green tops and set aside. Cut the white and light green sections into ¼-inch slices.

In a medium sauté pan, heat the olive oil over medium heat. Add the white and light green scallions and sauté for 3 to 5 minutes, or until the scallions are golden brown. Add the pepper and sun-dried tomato mixture and stir well to deglaze the pan. Bring to a boil, reduce the heat, and simmer for 15 minutes. Remove the pan from the heat and mash

the sauce well with a potato masher. Return to very low heat to keep warm while you prepare the pasta.

Cut the dark green scallion tops into ¼-inch slices and set aside.

Cook the angel hair al dente, according to the package directions. Drain well, rinse to remove starch, and drain again. Toss with the sauce, garnish with the scallion tops, and serve immediately.

MAKES 4 TO 6 SERVINGS

NOTE: This dish is not designed to be drowned in sauce. Rather, the pasta is seasoned by the sauce. If you really want it saucy, double the sauce ingredients or reduce the pasta quantity. I like a sauce with big chunks of sun-dried tomatoes that produce bursts of flavor. If you prefer smaller pieces, you can pulse the sauce to suit your taste in a blender or a food processor fitted with a chopping blade.

Hot Nutty Noodles

Looking for adventure? I love to ride and find someplace new to explore. I also love to do "adventure cooking," exploring new tastes and flavor combinations. So if you can't come for a ride with me, let's explore the kitchen together. This wild combination of ingredients may sound strange—who thinks of pasta and peanut butter together? Well, this recipe is an adventure for your taste buds. So gather the ingredients, fire up the stove, and take a ride on the wild side with this nutty noodle experience.

6 scallions

¼ cup peanut oil

2 fresh long slim red cayenne peppers, stemmed and minced

1 fresh red jalapeño pepper, stemmed and minced

7 garlic cloves, minced

½ cup unsalted roasted cashews, coarsely chopped

2 tablespoons sesame seeds

½ cup chunky peanut butter

1 cup coconut milk

¼ cup water

Salt and ground black pepper

1 pound angel hair pasta

Fill a large pot with water and bring to a boil to cook the pasta.

Trim the scallions. Remove the dark green tops, cut into ¼-inch-thick slices, and set aside. Mince the white and light green sections.

In a small saucepan, heat the peanut oil over low heat. Add the minced scallions, peppers, and garlic, the cashews, and sesame seeds and sauté for 3 to 5 minutes, or until the scallions are golden brown, being very careful not to burn the cashews and sesame seeds. Add the peanut butter and stir until completely melted. Add the coconut milk and stir well to blend. Slowly add the water, stirring constantly until well blended. Season with salt and pepper to taste.

continued

Keep the sauce warm over very low heat while you prepare the pasta, stirring often so it does not separate.

Cook the angel hair al dente, according to the package directions.

Just before serving, add the dark green pieces of scallion to the sauce and stir well.

Drain the pasta well and toss with the sauce. Serve immediately.

MAKES 4 TO 6 SERVINGS

Loco Lo Mein

This variation on a Chinese restaurant standard blends in a little Central American flavor with the ancho and New Mexico peppers. It's an easy dish to prepare, just lots of slicing and dicing and tossing in the pan. I've used bean curd, but you can substitute chicken, shrimp, pork, beef, or whatever—just adjust the cooking time as needed.

1 ancho pepper, stemmed, seeded, and torn into small
    pieces

1 dried New Mexico pepper, stemmed, seeded, and torn
    into small pieces

½ cup boiling water (see page 18)

2-inch length fresh ginger, peeled and julienned

1 broccoli stalk

¼ cup extra-virgin olive oil

1 pound extra-firm bean curd, drained and cut into
    ½-inch cubes

2 carrots, peeled and cut into ¼-inch slices

6 scallions

1 (8-ounce) can sliced water chestnuts, drained

1 (15-ounce) can baby corn, drained

1 cup sliced mushrooms

1 small zucchini, quartered lengthwise and cut into
    ½-inch pieces

1 red bell pepper, cored and julienned

1 cup snow peas, trimmed and cut into ½-inch pieces

2 tablespoons chopped garlic

½ cup light teriyaki sauce

1 teaspoon ground black pepper

1 (10-ounce) package Chinese noodles or 1 pound angel
    hair pasta

continued

Put the ancho and New Mexico peppers in a small bowl and cover with the boiling water. Place the ginger on top of the peppers and set aside to cool to room temperature.

Fill a large pot with water and bring to a boil to cook the noodles.

Remove the broccoli florets from the stalk. Break or cut the florets into bite-size pieces and set aside. Trim any leaves or hard dry parts from the broccoli stalk. Cut the stalk into ¼-inch slices.

Heat the olive oil in a very large sauté pan or wok over high heat. Add the bean curd and sauté for 8 to 10 minutes, or until the bean curd begins to brown. Add the broccoli stalks and carrots and sauté for 3 to 5 minutes, or until the carrots begin to brown.

While the carrots are sautéing, trim the scallions. Remove the dark green tops and set aside. Cut the white and light green sections into ¼-inch slices.

Add the white and light green scallions, water chestnuts, baby corn, mushrooms, zucchini, bell pepper, and snow peas to the pan and sauté for 3 to 5 minutes. Add the broccoli florets and sauté for 2 to 3 minutes, or until the florets turn dark green but are still crispy.

In a blender or food processor equipped with a chopping blade, combine the rehydrated peppers, ginger, garlic, teriyaki sauce, and black pepper. Puree for 1 minute, or until smooth.

Add the puree to the vegetables and stir well. Reduce the heat to low and simmer, covered, while you prepare the noodles.

Cook the noodles al dente, about 3 minutes (refer to the package directions for suggested cooking time).

While the noodles cook, thinly slice the dark green scallion tops.

Drain the noodles well and toss with the vegetables. Serve immediately, with the dark green scallion tops sprinkled on top.

MAKES 6 TO 8 SERVINGS

Joe Allen's Polka Pepper Pasta[*]

This recipe is the first winner of my Viewer Recipe Contest. Joe, who works building docks and piers in the New York City harbor, got this recipe from an old Polish sailor. According to the sailor, this is a very old Polish dish. Joe tells me he enjoys this pasta when he goes camping, and he can easily pack the ingredients in his Harley Electra Glide Ultra Classic. Sounds to me like Joe knows how to travel—a big bike on the open road, camping under the stars, and cooking with fire. Alright, Joe Allen!

½ cup (1 stick) margarine
3 fresh red jalapeño peppers, stemmed and thinly sliced
7 garlic cloves, thinly sliced
2 large sweet onions, quartered and cut into thick slices
1 medium head cabbage, quartered, cored, and cut into
    thick slices
Salt and ground black pepper
1 pound home-style egg noodles

Fill a large pot with water and bring to a boil to cook the noodles.

Melt the margarine in a very large sauté pan over medium heat. Add the jalapeño peppers, garlic, and onions. Add the cabbage until the pan is full. You may not be able to fit all the cabbage in the pan at first, but you can add more as it cooks down. Sauté, stirring often, for 15 to 20 minutes, or until all the cabbage is tender and transparent. Season with salt and black pepper to taste.

Cook the egg noodles al dente, according to the package directions. Drain well and transfer to a large serving bowl. Add the cabbage and mix well. Serve piping hot.

MAKES 6 TO 8 SERVINGS

Contest winner

Rowdy Ratatouille*

Now this is a winner. Start with a blend of Italian garden vegetables cooked into a wonderful chunky sauce. Combine that sauce with the texture of rotelle pasta, cover it with a layer of cheddar cheese, and look out! This dish is sure to satisfy the cravings of any hungry bikers you know, and before you ask for seconds holler "Alright!" as thanks to Daria and Liana Sellon for this tasty winner.

3 tablespoons extra-virgin olive oil

1 large onion, quartered and cut into thick slices

2 fresh red jalapeño peppers, stemmed and thinly sliced

1 red bell pepper, cored, quartered, and cut into thick slices

1 yellow bell pepper, cored, quartered, and cut into thick slices

1 medium eggplant, sliced into 1-inch rounds then cut into ½-inch wedges

2 small zucchini, halved lengthwise and cut into 1-inch pieces

1 cup thick-sliced mushrooms

1½ teaspoons dried oregano

2 tablespoons dried parsley

1½ teaspoons ground black pepper

1½ teaspoons salt

5 tablespoons chopped garlic

1 (28-ounce) can whole peeled tomatoes, coarsely chopped, with their juice

1 pound rotelle pasta

2 cups shredded cheddar cheese

Fill a large pot with water and bring to a boil to cook the pasta.

Heat the olive oil in a large sauté pan over medium heat. Add the onion, jalapeños, and bell peppers and stir to coat with oil. Sauté for 2 to 3 minutes, or until the onion is just tender. Add the eggplant, zucchini, and mushrooms and stir to coat with oil. Sauté for 6 to 8 minutes, or until the eggplant is tender. Add the oregano, parsley, black pepper, salt, garlic, and tomatoes and stir well. Bring to a boil, reduce the heat to low, and simmer for 6 to 10 minutes, or until the sauce thickens.

Preheat the oven to 350°F.

While the Rowdy Ratatouille simmers, cook the rotelle pasta al dente, according to the package directions.

Drain the pasta well. Transfer to a large baking dish and cover with the Rowdy Ratatouille. Sprinkle the cheese over the vegetables and bake for 10 to 12 minutes, or until the cheese is melted and bubbly.

MAKES ABOUT 6 SERVINGS

Contest winner

Stuffed Shells from Hell

While I was gassing up at a local service station, the mechanic walked up to me with a funny expression on his face. I assumed he was going to tell me something like "Hey, one of your tires is going flat." But instead he asked, "Aren't you Biker Billy?" As we talked I discovered that his son Chris worked at a bike shop where I have one of my motorcycles serviced. As the conversation progressed, Hank asked if I could cook something that was tasty but not hot. In response, I created this recipe, which is doubly hot—but still tasty even if you leave out the hot peppers. Alright, Hank Budnik!

> 2 fresh habanero peppers, stemmed and seeded
> 1 medium onion
> 1 bunch broccoli
> 1 tablespoon chopped garlic
> ½ teaspoon salt
> ½ teaspoon ground black pepper
> ½ teaspoon dried oregano
> 1 cup shredded mozzarella cheese, plus extra to taste for
>   the topping
> 1 cup ricotta cheese
> 1 cup grated Parmesan cheese
> 1 (12-ounce) box large shells
> Stuffed Shells from Hell Sauce (recipe follows)

In a food processor equipped with a chopping blade, chop the habaneros as fine as possible (this helps to spread their heat throughout the filling and prevents someone from getting too much in one bite). Trim, peel, and quarter the onion. Add to the food processor and chop fine. Remove the broccoli florets from the stalks and set aside. Trim any leaves or hard dry parts from the stalks and finely chop the stems in the food processor with the habaneros and onion. Add the florets and chop fine. The habaneros should be thoroughly mixed with the chopped broccoli.

Transfer the broccoli mixture to a large bowl. Add the garlic, salt, black pepper, and oregano, and mix well. Add the 1 cup mozzarella, the ricotta, and Parmesan to the bowl and mix thoroughly. Cover and place in the refrigerator for at least 1 hour. (You can prepare the recipe to this point a day ahead, if you like.)

Fill a large pot with water and bring to a boil. Cook the shells al dente, according to the package directions. Drain and rinse with cold water to stop the cooking process and remove excess starch. Allow the shells to drain thoroughly.

Prepare the Stuffed Shells from Hell Sauce.

Preheat the oven to 350°F.

Cover the bottom of a large baking dish with a thin layer of sauce. Fill each shell with a heaping tablespoon of the cheese mix. (Do not over-stuff them; you should be able to just close the shell around the cheese mix.) Arrange the stuffed shells on top of the sauce in a single layer. Cover with more sauce, but don't drown them. Sprinkle the remaining mozzarella cheese across the top.

Place in the preheated oven and bake 15 to 20 minutes, or until the cheese melts and starts to brown. Serve immediately.

MAKES ABOUT 8 SERVINGS

NOTE: You can mince the habaneros, broccoli, and onions by hand, if you like, but since these ingredients are not cooked before being combined with the cheeses, you will find that a food processor does the job of mincing and combining best. Besides, it is faster, so you have more time left to go for a ride.

continued

STUFFED SHELLS FROM HELL SAUCE

This sauce is also great on pizza or pasta.

1 or more cherry peppers, stemmed
1 medium onion
3 tablespoons extra-virgin olive oil
1 tablespoon chopped garlic
1 tablespoon dried parsley
Salt and ground black pepper
Dried oregano
1 (28-ounce) can whole peeled tomatoes

Finely chop the peppers in a food processor fitted with a chopping blade, or dice them by hand.

Trim, peel, and quarter the onion. Finely chop in the food processor, or dice by hand.

Heat the olive oil over medium heat in a large sauté pan. Add the chopped cherry pepper and onion and stir well. Add the chopped garlic and parsley. Season to taste with salt, black pepper, and oregano and sauté 3 to 5 minutes, or until the onions are golden brown.

Coarsely chop the tomatoes with their liquid in the food processor, or dice by hand, and add to the pan. Bring to a boil, reduce the heat, and simmer 5 to 10 minutes, or until the sauce starts to thicken. (Do not overcook, as this should be a chunky, fresh sauce.)

Adjust the seasonings to taste and use the sauce as directed in the stuffed shells recipe.

Maniacal Manicotti

After just one forkful of this manicotti, you will probably require a strait-jacket to keep from eating a whole plateful. The jalapeño-powered sauce alone is enough to drive you crazy. But when you add the manicotti stuffed with this insanely delicious cheese filling, the mania begins. The choice is yours—close the book and ride away now, or start cooking and fall under the spell of the habanero-fired manicotti from hell.

> 1 ancho pepper, stemmed, seeded, and torn into small
> pieces
> 6 sun-dried tomatoes, thinly sliced
> 4 teaspoons chopped garlic
> 1 dried habanero pepper, stemmed and seeded
> 1 cup boiling water (see page 18)
> 3 tablespoons extra-virgin olive oil
> 1 large onion, diced
> 1 cup shredded mozzarella cheese, plus extra to taste for
> the topping
> 2 cups ricotta cheese
> ½ cup grated Parmesan and Romano cheeses
> 2 tablespoons dried parsley
> Maniacal Sauce (recipe follows)
> 1 (8-ounce) package manicotti pasta

Combine the ancho pepper, sun-dried tomatoes, garlic, and habanero pepper in a small heatproof bowl and cover with boiling water. Set aside and allow to cool to room temperature.

Heat 2 tablespoons of olive oil in a small sauté pan over medium heat. Add the onion and sauté 3 to 5 minutes, or until golden brown. Add the pepper and sun-dried tomato mixture and bring to a boil. Reduce the heat and simmer 2 to 4 minutes, or until all the liquid is absorbed. Remove from the heat and allow to cool to room temperature.

Combine the rehydrated pepper mixture and the remaining tablespoon of olive oil in a blender or a food processor equipped with a chop-

ping blade. Puree for 1 to 2 minutes, until the mixture is smooth and contains no solid pieces.

Combine 1 cup of the mozzarella, the ricotta, and Parmesan and Romano cheeses in a large bowl. Add the parsley and the pureed mixture and blend well to thoroughly combine. Refrigerate the cheese mixture while you prepare the sauce and pasta.

Prepare the Maniacal Sauce.

Fill a large pot with water and bring to a boil. Cook the manicotti al dente according to the package directions. (It is best to undercook them slightly so that they remain firm and will not become soggy when baked in the sauce.) Drain and rinse gently with cold water to stop the cooking process and remove excess starch. Let cool to room temperature.

Preheat the oven to 350°F.

Cover the bottom of a large baking dish with some of the sauce. Stuff each manicotti with the cheese mixture. (You can use a pastry bag with a plain tube to fill the manicotti. Or, what I do is simply use a small spoon to gently stuff some cheese into one end, then place that end on the counter and fill from the other side. Piping the filling into the manicotti is the "gourmet way," but you can use any technique or tool that works for you.) Arrange the stuffed manicotti on top of the sauce in a single layer. Cover with more sauce and the remaining mozzarella.

Place in the preheated oven and bake for 15 to 20 minutes, or until the cheese is melted and begins to brown. Serve hot.

MAKES 12 TO 14 MANICOTTI

MANIACAL SAUCE

2 tablespoons extra-virgin olive oil

**2 or more fresh red jalapeño peppers, stemmed,
    quartered lengthwise, and thinly sliced**

1 large onion, diced

4 teaspoons chopped garlic

1 teaspoon dried oregano

1 teaspoon salt

1 teaspoon ground black pepper

2 tablespoons dried parsley

**1 (28-ounce) can whole peeled tomatoes, coarsely
    chopped, with their juice**

Heat the olive oil in a large sauté pan over medium heat. Add the jalapeños, onion, and garlic and stir to coat with oil. Sauté for 3 to 5 minutes, or until the onions are golden brown. Add the oregano, salt, black pepper, parsley, and tomatoes. Bring to a boil, reduce the heat, and simmer for 8 to 10 minutes, or until the sauce just thickens. (You don't want to overcook it. The short cooking time helps to create a fresher tasting sauce.) Use as directed in the manicotti recipe.

Tortured Tortellini

This recipe will bring out the culinary sadomasochist that lurks in your kitchen. It's not the heat, it's the tiny tortellini that may torture you. The smaller the tortellini, the thinner the dough, the more careful the assembly, the more exquisite the dining experience. That means you have to make so many more of these delicious devils to fill the same size portion. As if that weren't enough, once you taste them you just have to have more and more. Soon the whole household is in the kitchen, torturing themselves by making and eating tortellini. So put on your leathers, grab your apron, and let the flour fly as you run to the kitchen yelling, "ALRIGHT, let's torture the tortellini!"

The recipe has two main components: the cheese filling and the pasta dough. For the cheese filling there are two variations to choose from: Red Fire Cheese Stuffing (below) or Green Fire Cheese Stuffing (page 137).

First select and prepare the cheese stuffing. While the stuffing chills, prepare the dough. While the dough is resting, bring the cooking water to a boil and prepare your assembly area. The tortellini are best when served immediately, so prepare the sauce and the rest of the meal before boiling the tortellini. Try topping them with Tortured Sun-Dried Tomato Sauce on page 137.

RED FIRE CHEESE STUFFING

Cruising down the culinary superhighway, you see flashing red lights in your taste buds' mirror. Are you about to be stopped for excessive pleasure? No way, it's just them old chipotle peppers smoking up your tongue. Use this fiery cheese stuffing in the Tortured Tortellini and you might just earn a citation.

½ cup shredded low-moisture mozzarella cheese
½ cup part-skim ricotta cheese
¼ cup grated Parmesan cheese

6 sun-dried tomatoes

2 chipotle peppers packed in adobo sauce

¼ cup boiling water (see page 18)

¼ cup diced red bell pepper

½ cup plain bread crumbs

¼ teaspoon salt

¼ teaspoon ground black pepper

Combine the three cheeses in a large bowl and mix well. Cover and refrigerate until needed.

Put the sun-dried tomatoes and chipotle peppers in a small bowl and cover with the boiling water. Set aside and allow to cool to room temperature.

In a blender or food processor equipped with a chopping blade, puree the rehydrated tomatoes and peppers with the bell pepper for 30 seconds to 1 minute, until smooth. Combine the puree with the cheese mixture and the remaining ingredients and blend well.

Cover and refrigerate for 30 minutes, or until needed.

MAKES 2 TO 3 CUPS

PASTA DOUGH

1⅓ cups all-purpose flour, plus additional flour for rolling
   the dough

2 large eggs

1 teaspoon salt

2 teaspoons olive oil, plus additional oil for kneading the
   dough

2 tablespoons water

Place 1⅓ cups of flour on a large glass plate (or in a large bowl), forming a mound with a well in the center. The well should be large enough to hold the eggs, oil, and water, and there should be flour at the bottom of the well.

Put the eggs in the well and sprinkle the salt on top of the eggs. Add the 2 teaspoons of olive oil and the water. Using a fork, slowly mix the

flour from the outside of the plate into the well, stirring until the mixture becomes a dough. Cover your hands with additional olive oil and knead the dough until it stops sticking to you fingers (you may need to add a little more flour). Form the dough into a ball, cover, and let rest for 10 minutes.

TORTURED TORTELLINI ASSEMBLY

Divide the dough into 4 pieces. (When rolled, these should produce manageable size sheets of dough.) Using a floured rolling pin on a floured surface, roll the dough, one piece at a time, into a rectangle about ⅛ inch thick. Roll from the center toward the outside, and turn the dough a quarter turn between each rolling. Always make sure there is enough flour on the rolling pin and surface to prevent sticking.

Cut the rolled dough into 2-inch squares (this measurement can be varied to produce larger or smaller tortellini). Place a spoonful of cheese stuffing in the center of each square (the size of "spoonful" should be adjusted according to the size of the pasta square). There should be an even border of pasta around the filling wide enough to allow you to easily seal the edges. Pick up one corner of the pasta and fold it over the filling, creating a triangle. Pinch the edges closed. It is important that the filling be completely sealed inside the pasta. Pick up the pasta triangle, holding it by the two corners that are connected by the fold. Gently bring the two corners together so that they overlap, and pinch them together. Place the assembled tortellini on a floured plate. Be careful they do not touch each other, or they will stick together. Repeat until all the tortellini are assembled.

Fill a large pot with water. While you assemble the tortellini, bring the water to a rolling boil. Drop the tortellini into the boiling water a few at a time while gently stirring with a wooden spoon. (By adding the tortellini a few at a time the water should remain at a rolling boil, and the stirring should prevent them from sticking to the pot or each other.) Cooking time is determined by the thickness of the dough and your preference for a firm or soft pasta. The tortellini will cook quickly (1 to 5 minutes) and float to the top when done. The only way to know if they are done is to test one by eating it; start testing as soon as most of them are floating near the top. It is better to err on the side of firmness.

Drain the tortellini thoroughly and serve immediately, with Tortured Sun-Dried Tomato Sauce, if you like.

MAKES ABOUT THIRTY 2-INCH TORTELLINI

GREEN FIRE CHEESE STUFFING

As the traffic light turns green, you smoothly release the clutch while opening the throttle. Each light you approach flashes to green and the road is yours. Up through the gears you shift, power and speed flowing from the machine into your very soul. There is no other sensation like riding your bike down the boulevard as green traffic lights run off into the distance. The feeling of freedom wells up in your throat; this is what life is all about. You have just tasted the "green fire." Stuff your Tortured Tortellini (page 134) with this mix and let's roll!

½ cup shredded low-moisture mozzarella cheese
½ cup part-skim ricotta cheese
¼ cup grated Parmesan cheese
2 fresh green serrano peppers, stemmed, seeded, and
    minced
1 packed cup fresh spinach, minced
¼ teaspoon salt
¼ teaspoon ground black pepper

Combine the three cheeses in a large mixing bowl and mix well. Add the remaining ingredients and mix again until completely blended.

Cover and refrigerate for 30 minutes, or until needed.

TORTURED SUN-DRIED TOMATO SAUCE

Ancient friends flung far apart by adventure and conquest. The hot sun beats down on one laid out on a rack. Meanwhile, halfway around the world, the other is hung up in a smokehouse. Both are destined to meet a dry end. What kinds of cruel torture will these friends endure as they ride to find each other? But when they are united and revived, what a

celebration to behold! Two native Americans—the tomato, sun-dried, and the chipotle, a smoked jalapeño—ride together in this adventurous sauce; let it conquer your appetite. Try it with Tortured Tortellini (page 134) or your favorite pasta.

3 chipotle peppers packed in adobo sauce, minced
12 sun-dried tomatoes, minced
1 cup boiling water (see page 18)
¼ cup extra-virgin olive oil
2 medium onions, julienned
3 tablespoons chopped garlic
1 red bell pepper, cored and julienned
2 Italian frying peppers, cored and julienned
½ teaspoon salt
½ teaspoon coarsely ground black pepper

Put the chipotle peppers and sun-dried tomatoes in a small bowl and cover with the boiling water. Set aside and allow to cool to room temperature.

Heat the olive oil in a large sauté pan over medium heat. Add the onions, garlic, bell pepper, and Italian peppers and sauté for 3 to 5 minutes, or until the onions are golden. Add the salt, black pepper, and rehydrated chipotles and sun-dried tomatoes to the pan. Bring to a boil, reduce the heat to low, and simmer for about 10 minutes, or until the sauce thickens. Serve hot.

Peppered Pirogi

Spend a few weeks motorcycle touring and camping, away from the hurly-burly of big-city life, and you develop a real appreciation for simple pleasures. A sunny day is so special after a week of riding in the rain. These peppered pirogi—fresh pasta packed with a creamy blend of potatoes and cheese—are like that sunny day, a simple pleasure worth savoring. Fire from the serrano peppers adds a warm edge to these Eastern European delights. Added to soups, sautéed in margarine, or deep fried—however you serve them, they will become one of your simple pleasures.

> 3 fresh serrano peppers, stemmed
> 4 cups peeled 1-inch potato chunks
> 3 tablespoons margarine
> 6 tablespoons half-and-half
> 1 teaspoon salt
> 1½ cups shredded cheddar cheese
> Pirogi Dough (recipe follows)
> Sour cream

Put the serranos and potatoes in a large saucepan. Cover with water and bring to a boil over high heat. Reduce the heat and simmer for about 10 minutes, or until the potatoes are tender.

Using a slotted spoon, remove the serranos from the saucepan; set aside. Drain the potatoes, reserving the water.

Place the serranos in a food processor equipped with a chopping blade and process for 30 seconds, or until chopped fine. Add the potatoes, margarine, half-and-half, and salt to the food processor and process for 30 seconds. Scrape down the sides of the food processor and add the cheese. Process for about 3 minutes, or until the mixture is smooth and creamy. Transfer to a bowl, cover, and set aside to cool.

Prepare the Pirogi Dough.

Place a couple of spoonfuls of the potato-cheese mixture in the center of each dough circle. There should be a margin of dough as wide as

your thumb around the filling. (There should be no filling on this margin or the dough won't seal.) Fold the dough in half over the filling and press the overlapping edges of the dough together. (Be sure to seal the edges well or they will come apart when you cook them.) Set the finished pirogi on a floured plate so they don't touch each other and sprinkle with flour. Let them sit for a few minutes to firm up.

In a large saucepan, combine the water the potatoes were cooked in with enough additional water to fill the pot up to 2 or 3 inches from the top. Bring to a boil. Drop the pirogi into the boiling water a few at a time and cook for 2 to 3 minutes, until they float. Remove with a slotted spoon and drain thoroughly. Serve them immediately, with sour cream. They also taste fantastic fried in margarine until golden brown after they have been boiled.

MAKES EIGHTEEN 4-INCH PIROGI

Pirogi Dough

2 cups all-purpose flour, plus additional flour for rolling the dough

3 extra-large eggs

1½ teaspoons salt

1 tablespoon olive oil, plus additional oil for kneading the dough

3 tablespoons water

Place 2 cups of flour on a large glass plate (or in a large bowl), forming a mound with a well in the center. The well should be large enough to hold the eggs, oil, and water, and there should be flour at the bottom of the well.

Put the eggs in the well and sprinkle the salt on top of the eggs. Add the tablespoon of olive oil and the water. Using a fork, slowly mix the flour from the outside of the plate into the well, stirring until the mixture become a dough. Cover your hands with additional olive oil and knead the dough until it stops sticking to you fingers (you may need to add a little more flour). Form the dough into a ball, cover, and let rest for 10 minutes.

Shape the ball of dough into a long roll about 1 inch in diameter. Cut the roll into 18 pieces. Form each piece into a small ball, sprinkle with flour, and set aside while you make the remaining balls.

Using a floured rolling pin on a floured surface, roll the small dough balls, one at a time, into 4-inch circles about $\frac{1}{8}$ to $\frac{1}{4}$ inch thick. They are now ready for stuffing according to the pirogi recipe.

Big Bikes: Main Dishes

CALL THEM big bikes, tourers, or dressers, these machines are long-range travelers. You'll see them on the highway, decked out with saddlebags, trunks, and all sorts of storage pockets to hold everything needed for weeks on the road. Add a comfortable saddle, highway boards to stretch your legs, a stereo to sing along with, and a CB to talk with fellow travelers, and you're ready for anything. Whether weekend wandering or cross-country bound, a big bike will get you there in style and comfort, providing more fun per mile than any other form of travel.

But strip down a big dresser, shedding all the chrome and bags, and you will find at the heart a big motor in a solid frame. Dinner is the same—remove all the side dishes, appetizers, soups, and desserts and what is left is the main dish. It provides the character of the meal. Some of the recipes in this chapter are meals in themselves, others need side dishes. You decide for yourself. Some people strip down dressers so they can enjoy the pleasure of a powerful motor, others like all the extras. Alright, dinner's ready, come and get it!

Smoky Bean Curd Stir-Fry

Cut up the vegetables as you cook the stir-fry—the order in which the ingredients are added ensures that the veggies will have the perfect texture when finished. Remember, a stir-fry needs to be stirred often.

> 1 (3.75-ounce) bag bean thread (cellophane) noodles
> 1 to 2 large broccoli stalks
> 7 scallions
> Peanut or olive oil
> 2 or more fresh serrano peppers, stemmed and thinly sliced
> 6 or more garlic cloves, coarsely chopped
> 1-inch cube fresh ginger, peeled and minced
> 4 carrots, peeled and cut into irregularly shaped pieces
> 3 celery stalks, sliced ¾ inch thick on a bias
> 1 pound extra-firm bean curd, drained
> Liquid Smoke
> 1 small zucchini, quartered lengthwise and cut into ¼-inch slices
> 1 cup snow peas, trimmed
> 1 (15-ounce) can baby corn, drained
> 1 red bell pepper, cored and cut into ¾-inch squares
> Salt and ground black pepper

Bring a large pot of water to a boil. Add the bean threads, stir, then remove from heat and set aside to soak; they should be ready when the stir-fry is done. (If the package directions are different, follow them.)

Trim the broccoli, removing the florets and breaking them into bite-size pieces; set aside. Cut the stalks into irregular chunks (rotating the stalk between cuts and changing the angle of the cut). Trim the scallions. Remove the dark green tops and set aside. Cut the white and light green sections into ¾-inch-thick slices. Thinly slice the dark green sections.

Heat several tablespoons of oil in a very large sauté pan or wok. (It may be necessary to add more oil as you add more ingredients.) Put the

serrano peppers, garlic, and ginger into the sauté pan or wok. Stir-fry for 1 minute. Add the broccoli stalk and carrots and stir well to coat with oil. Stir-fry for 3 minutes. Add the white and light green sections of the scallions along with the celery to the sauté pan or wok and stir-fry for 2 minutes.

Place the bean curd on a cutting board with large side up. Cut on diagonals into 4 triangles, then place each triangular piece on its longest side and cut in half from tip toward the longest side. Slice each triangular chunk into 4 slices. Place the bean curd pieces in the hot oil a few at a time, stirring to coat with oil. Stir-fry until the bean curd begins to brown, 6 to 8 minutes. Add several generous dashes of Liquid Smoke while stirring. (Use as much as you like, but taste a small piece of bean curd to judge. You can add more Liquid Smoke as you go.)

Add the zucchini, snow peas, baby corn, and bell pepper to the sauté pan or wok. Stir in the broccoli florets and the dark green scallion tops, then stir-fry until the florets start to turn dark green, about 2 minutes.

Drain and rinse the bean threads. In a very large serving bowl, toss together the bean threads and stir-fried mixture. Serve immediately.

MAKES ABOUT 6 SERVINGS

Mixed Bag Parmigiana

I love spending a day riding demo bikes at a big motorcycle rally. At these events, every manufacturer turns up with every type of motorcycle, from sport bikes and big touring rigs to cruisers and sidecars. It is so much fun to try a few miles on each type of bike. You really get a taste for all the ways of enjoying the world's most fantastic sport.

When I cook I also like to indulge myself with variety (and it is a lot cheaper in the kitchen than in the bike shop). This recipe is prepared in three steps. First you make the sauce, then the vegetables are breaded and fried. Finally the dish is assembled and baked. The complex mix of flavors offers plenty of variety.

SAUCE

2 dried long slim cayenne peppers, stemmed and crushed

1 ancho pepper, stemmed, seeded, and torn into small pieces

½ cup boiling water (see page 18)

Olive oil

3 garlic cloves, crushed

2 medium onions, coarsely chopped

1 (28-ounce) can crushed tomatoes

Salt and ground black pepper

Dried oregano

VEGETABLES

1 large broccoli stalk

Corn chips, coarsely ground

Pancake mix (enough to make 10 pancakes)

Olive oil, for frying

1 summer squash, sliced into ½-inch rounds

1 small eggplant, sliced into ½-inch rounds

1 zucchini, sliced into ½-inch rounds

TO ASSEMBLE:

1 cup shredded mozzarella cheese, or more to taste

1 cup shredded mild cheddar cheese, or more to taste

To prepare the sauce: Place the cayenne and ancho peppers in a small bowl and cover with boiling water. Allow to cool to room temperature. Puree the peppers and water in a blender or food processor equipped with a chopping blade.

Heat several tablespoons of olive oil in a large sauté pan over medium heat. Add the pureed peppers, garlic, and onions and simmer for 2 to 3 minutes, or until the onions are transparent. Add the tomatoes and stir well. Add salt, black pepper, and oregano to taste. Simmer the sauce over low heat for 10 to 15 minutes. Don't overcook; the sauce is fresher tasting with less cooking. Remove from the heat and set aside.

To prepare the vegetables: Remove the stalk from the broccoli and set aside. Break the florets into pieces a little larger than bite-size. Trim and peel the stalk and cut lengthwise into ½-inch-thick slices.

Place the corn chip crumbs in a wide, shallow bowl that is larger than the biggest piece of prepared vegetable.

Prepare the pancake mix according to package directions. Transfer the batter to another wide, shallow bowl.

Heat ½ inch of oil in a large frying pan over medium heat.

Coat each piece of vegetable with the pancake batter and then roll in the corn chip crumbs. Put the breaded vegetables into the frying pan and fry for 3 to 5 minutes, or until the edges begin to turn golden brown. Carefully turn the breaded vegetables over and fry the other side until golden brown. (It may be necessary to add more oil as you work.) Drain well on paper towels.

To assemble the parmigiana: Preheat the oven to 350°F.

Cover the bottom of a large baking dish with a little sauce. Add a layer of breaded fried vegetables and cover lightly with sauce. Add a generous

layer of cheeses. (You can prepare this as a single-layer dish or in multiple layers.) Bake until the cheese is completely melted and bubbly brown, 15 to 20 minutes. Serve piping hot.

MAKES ABOUT 8 SERVINGS

Spanakopita Diablo

The spinach pie from hell, this tastes so good it has to be sinful. A crispy golden crust made of phyllo dough encases a fiery combination of spinach and feta cheese. This dish is a favorite of mine, and I am sure it will be a favorite of yours. Although this is a main dish, it is equally welcome at lunch or cut into small pieces as an appetizer. Serve it and tell everybody the devil made you do it.

> 2 tablespoons olive oil
>
> 3 fresh long slim red cayenne peppers, stemmed and minced
>
> 6 garlic cloves, minced
>
> 2 medium onions, minced
>
> 2 (10-ounce) packages frozen chopped spinach, thawed and drained, liquid reserved (see Note)
>
> 2 tablespoons dried parsley
>
> 8 ounces feta cheese, crumbled
>
> 1/4 teaspoon ground nutmeg
>
> 1/2 teaspoon salt
>
> 1/2 teaspoon ground black pepper
>
> 2 jumbo eggs, lightly beaten
>
> 1/2 cup melted margarine, or more as needed
>
> 8 ounces frozen phyllo dough, thawed (see page 21)

Heat the oil in a small sauté pan over medium heat. Put in the cayenne peppers, garlic, and onions and sauté for about 3 minutes, or until the onions are transparent. Add the reserved spinach liquid and the parsley and simmer for about 3 minutes, or until the liquid is almost gone. Remove from heat and set aside to cool.

In a large mixing bowl, combine the chopped spinach, feta cheese, nutmeg, salt, and black pepper. Add the cooled pepper mixture and eggs, then stir well to combine. Set aside.

Preheat the oven to 350°F.

continued

Generously brush an $8 \times 12\frac{1}{2} \times 1\frac{1}{4}$-inch pan with melted margarine. Lay a sheet of phyllo in the pan and brush it with melted margarine. Adding 1 sheet at a time, brushing each with melted margarine, use half the phyllo on the bottom of the pan, arranging sheets so they extend 1 inch beyond the top edge of the pan. Pour the spinach mixture into the pan and spread evenly. Fold the dough that is hanging out of the pan over the top of the mixture, and brush the top with melted margarine.

Cover the mixture with additional phyllo sheets one at a time, brushing each with melted margarine. Use all the phyllo. Brush the top with the remaining margarine (you want a good amount on the top because this yields a beautiful golden brown color), then bake for 1 hour.

Cut into triangular pieces and serve with rice and salad. If you have leftovers, reheat in the oven because the crust will lose its texture in the microwave.

MAKES 8 SERVINGS

NOTE: Frozen spinach holds a lot of liquid so I often find it is necessary to press the liquid out when it thaws. If you prefer to use 1 pound of fresh spinach, add 1 cup of water to replace the liquid reserved from the frozen spinach. Fresh spinach should be rinsed, drained, and dried, then chopped into small pieces (do this by hand, as a food processor will overchop).

Fire Foo Young

This is a great recipe to prepare when you're expecting a pack of hungry bikers. Just throw in more vegetables as the crowd grows. Cook up a big pot of rice, get your wok fired up, and when you hear the sound of bikes approaching, shout "Alright, come and get it while it's hot!"

FIRE SAUCE

¼ cup olive or peanut oil
1-inch cube fresh ginger, peeled and minced
3 fresh long slim red cayenne peppers, stemmed and minced
6 garlic cloves, minced
6 scallions, minced
½ cup light teriyaki sauce

OMELETS

6 scallions
1 broccoli stalk
¼ cup peanut oil, plus extra for frying omelets
3 green Anaheim peppers, stemmed, seeded, and minced
6 garlic cloves, minced
1 (8-ounce) can sliced water chestnuts, drained
2 carrots, peeled and shredded
2 celery stalks, sliced ¾ inch thick on a bias
1 red bell pepper, cored and cut into ½-inch squares
1 yellow bell pepper, cored and cut into ½-inch squares
1 (15-ounce) can baby corn pieces, drained
16 large eggs
Liquid Smoke
Cooked rice

continued

To make the sauce: In a small saucepan, heat the oil over medium heat. Add the ginger, cayenne peppers, garlic, and scallions, and simmer until tender, about 3 minutes. Reduce the heat to low, add the teriyaki sauce, and simmer, covered, for 30 minutes. You may need to add some water to replace any liquid that is lost during cooking.

To make the omelets: Trim the scallions. Remove the dark green tops, cut into ¼-inch-thick slices, and set aside. Cut the white and light green sections into ¼-inch-thick slices. Trim the broccoli. Remove the florets, break into bite-size pieces, and set aside. Cut the stalk into irregular chunks (rotating the stalk between cuts and changing the angle of the cut).

Place a large wok over high heat. Pour the ¼ cup oil into the wok and swirl it around to cover the surface. The oil is hot enough when a small piece of vegetable begins to sizzle as soon as it is added to the oil. As you stir-fry ingredients in the wok, move what is already in the wok to the sides and let the oil drain to the bottom. Place the new ingredient in the center and stir to cover with oil, then stir all the ingredients together.

Place the white and light green sections of the scallions, the Anaheim peppers, and the garlic in the wok. Toss to coat with oil and stir-fry for 1 minute. Add the broccoli stalk pieces to the wok and stir-fry for 1 minute. Add the water chestnuts and stir-fry for 1 minute. Add the carrots and stir-fry for 1 minute. Add the celery and stir-fry for 1 minute. Add the red and yellow bell peppers and stir-fry for 1 minute. Add the baby corn pieces and stir-fry for 1 minute. Finally, add the broccoli florets and dark green scallion tops. Stir-fry until the broccoli florets turn dark green and are still crisp, about 2 minutes. Remove the vegetables from the wok, and place in a strainer over a bowl to allow the excess oil to drain.

In a large mixing bowl, beat 2 eggs with several dashes of Liquid Smoke. Add some of the vegetables to the beaten eggs. (There should be more egg than vegetable in this mixture or the omelet will not hold together.)

Heat enough oil to coat the wok over a high heat; you may have to add a little oil before frying each additonal omelet. Pour the egg and vegetable mixture into the center of the wok. Cook until the eggs are firm, turn over, and brown the other side. Transfer to a plate

and keep warm. Repeat the omelet preparation until all 8 omelets are cooked.

For each serving, make a bed of rice on a plate and place an omelet on top. Stir the fire sauce well and spoon over the omelet to taste.

MAKES 8 OMELETS

Killer Curry

The first time I made this dish I was camping in a fog-enshrouded pullout along the Pacific Coast Highway a little north of San Simeon. For dinner I whipped up a tasty curry using canned ingredients and some spices that were in my saddlebags. The sound of the surf pounding against the cliffs and the blanket of dense fog made that curry the most memorable dinner of that journey. When I got home I tried to re-create that meal and this is the recipe. (Of course, at home I had the luxury of better ingredients and more equipment.) Close your eyes and listen carefully—you may hear the surf pounding against the cliffs. Serve over hot cooked rice.

1 (19-ounce) can garbanzo beans, drained, liquid
    reserved
2 (10-ounce) packages frozen chopped spinach
4 tablespoons (½ stick) margarine
2 fresh long slim red cayenne peppers, stemmed and
    minced
1 fresh red jalapeño pepper, stemmed and minced
7 garlic cloves, minced
3 medium onions, minced
2 carrots, peeled, halved lengthwise, and cut into ½-inch
    slices
½ cup slivered almonds
½ cup golden raisins
2 teaspoons ground cumin
1 teaspoon ground coriander
1 teaspoon turmeric
1 tablespoon paprika
2 teaspoons salt
1 teaspoon ground black pepper
¼ teaspoon ground ginger
1 cup water
1 yellow bell pepper, cored and cut into ½-inch squares
⅔ cup coconut milk

In a large saucepan, combine the liquid from the garbanzo beans and the frozen spinach. Place over low heat, cover, and allow the spinach to thaw.

In a large sauté pan, melt the margarine over medium heat. Add the hot peppers, garlic, and onions and sauté for 1 minute. Add the carrots and sauté for 4 to 6 minutes, or until the onions are golden brown.

Stir in the slivered almonds, golden raisins, and garbanzo beans and stir well. Sauté for 1 minute. Add the cumin, coriander, turmeric, paprika, salt, black pepper, and ground ginger. Stir well and sauté for 1 minute. Add the thawed spinach with garbanzo liquid and water to the sauté pan, stir well, and simmer for 10 minutes.

Add the bell pepper and coconut milk to the sauté pan and stir well. Reduce the heat to low and simmer, covered, for 30 minutes. Serve piping hot with rice.

MAKES 4 TO 6 SERVINGS

Hot Pepper Pot Pie

Commercial pot pies are so bland. But who doesn't love a rich, flaky crust surrounding a hearty filling? Well, I have kick-started this tired dish into the fast lane. Start with three kinds of cheese and lots of tasty vegetables. Add two kinds of hot peppers and a rich smoky sauce. Wrap it up in an easy pie crust, and you're ready to kick into high gear for a taste adventure.

> 1 bunch broccoli
> 1 fresh red jalapeño pepper, stemmed
> 1 fresh green or red serrano pepper, stemmed
> 7 garlic cloves
> 3 medium onions
> 2 tablespoons margarine
> 3 medium red potatoes, cut into ½-inch cubes
> 2 carrots, peeled and cut into ½-inch slices
> 1 red bell pepper, cored and cut into 1-inch squares
> 1 yellow bell pepper, cored and cut into 1-inch squares
> ¼ cup half-and-half
> ½ teaspoon salt
> ½ teaspoon ground black pepper
> Liquid Smoke (optional)
> 1 package pie crust mix for a double-crust 9-inch pie
> 1 cup cubed cheddar cheese, in ½-inch pieces
> ½ cup cubed Swiss cheese, in ½-inch pieces
> ½ cup cubed muenster cheese, in ½-inch pieces

Trim the broccoli, discarding the stalks. Break the florets into bite-size pieces and set aside. Finely chop the jalapeño, serrano, and garlic in a food processor equipped with a chopping blade or in a blender. Trim, peel, and quarter the onions, then add to food processor or blender. Process until the onions are pureed; set aside. (If you are using a blender, it may be necessary to coarsely chop the onions before processing.)

In a large frying pan, melt the margarine over high heat. Put the pota-

toes and carrots into the frying pan and fry for 5 to 8 minutes, or until the potatoes are golden brown.

Add the broccoli florets and bell peppers and stir well. Reduce the heat to low. Add the pureed hot peppers, garlic, and onions and stir well. Simmer for 2 to 3 minutes, or until the broccoli starts to turn dark green but is still crispy. Stir in the half-and-half, salt, black pepper, and several dashes of Liquid Smoke. Stir well and remove from the heat. Allow to cool while you prepare the pie crusts.

Preheat the oven to 450°F. The pie crust mix you use may recommend a different temperature; if so, use that temperature (see Note).

Prepare the pie crust according to package directions for 1 double-crust 9-inch pie. Put one crust into a 9-inch deep-dish pie pan. Add the cheese cubes to the vegetables and toss to combine. Transfer the mixture to the lined pie pan. This should fill the crust and then some. Form the filling into a dome shape. Lay the second crust on top and fold excess dough under the edge of the bottom crust and flute the edge with a fork. Poke several holes in the top crust so steam can escape while baking.

Bake for 30 minutes. The crust should be golden brown. Remove the pie from the oven and let cool on a raised pie rack for 10 to 15 minutes before serving. The cooling time allows the cheese to solidify enough to cut the pie into slices that will retain their "slice of pie" shape when served.

MAKES ONE 9-INCH PIE OR 4 TO 6 SERVINGS

NOTE: The baking time and temperature can be adjusted to accommodate any brand of pie crust. Remember—all ovens are different, so check the pie often and remove from the oven when the crust is golden brown.

Could Be Quiche

Real men don't eat quiche, so the saying goes. Well, real bikers eat anything they want, and this recipe is sure to please real bikers (male and female). The jalapeños, onion, and garlic give this dish that special biker attitude. Combine that attitude with the jack cheese and spinach, and you have a dish that a French gourmet would envy. Just remember to keep the French gourmets out of the kitchen, or it could be quiche.

    2 tablespoons margarine
    2 fresh red jalapeño peppers, stemmed, quartered
        lengthwise, and thinly sliced
    1 large onion, quartered and thinly sliced
    4 teaspoons chopped garlic
    3 large eggs
    1 package pie crust mix for a double-crust 9-inch pie
    1 (10-ounce) package frozen chopped spinach, thawed
        and drained well (see Note)
    1 cup half-and-half
    3 cups shredded Monterey jack cheese
    1 tablespoon paprika
    1 teaspoon salt
    1 teaspoon ground black pepper

Melt the margarine in a small sauté pan over medium heat. Add the jalapeños and onion and sauté for 2 to 3 minutes, or until the onion is transparent. Add the garlic, stir well, and remove from the heat; allow to cool to room temperature.

Separate the white from 1 egg and set aside. Beat the egg yolk with the other 2 eggs and set aside.

Preheat the oven to 375°F. (see Note, page 157).

Prepare the pie crust mix according to package directions for 2 single-crust 9-inch pies. Place the crusts in two 9-inch pie pans, pinch to flute the edges, and brush with the reserved egg white.

In a large mixing bowl, combine the spinach with the sautéed jala-

peños, onion, and garlic; toss together well. Add the half-and-half, cheese, paprika, salt and black pepper, and beaten eggs. Mix well. Divide the filling mixture between the 2 pie crusts. Bake for 45 minutes, or until a fork inserted in the center of the pie comes out clean. Serve warm, not hot, to help the filling keep its "piece of pie" shape.

MAKES TWO 9-INCH PIES OR 8 TO 12 SERVINGS

NOTE: Frozen spinach holds a lot of liquid, so I often find it is necessary to press the liquid out when it thaws. If you prefer to substitute ½ pound fresh spinach, it should be rinsed, drained, and dried, then chopped into small pieces (you will want to do this by hand as a food processor will overchop).

Not Just Fried Rice

Most fried rice is pretty basic; however, the take-out kind travels well, which is a plus for a hungry biker with room in his or her saddlebags. But this is far superior to takeout, and you can take it riding if you wish— but watch out for the sauce in those saddlebags.

Everyone I have served this dish to has enjoyed the sauce tremendously, so you may wish to double the sauce recipe.

You can prepare the fried rice part of the recipe without the cayenne peppers, and put extra hot peppers in the sauce. This way you can adjust the heat for each serving. After all, some people may even enjoy just the fried rice.

HOT LEEK SAUCE

1 tablespoon cornstarch

½ cup cool water

¼ cup peanut oil

1 leek, minced

½-inch cube fresh ginger, peeled and minced

1 or more fresh long slim red cayenne peppers, stemmed
  and minced

1 tablespoon chopped garlic

¼ cup light teriyaki sauce

RICE

¼ cup peanut oil

1-inch cube fresh ginger, peeled and minced

2 fresh long slim red cayenne peppers, stemmed and
  minced

6 scallions, minced

1 tablespoon chopped garlic

16 ounces extra-firm bean curd, drained and cut into
    ½-inch cubes

1 cup unsalted cashews

2 carrots, peeled and shredded

2 celery stalks, thinly sliced crosswise

1 cup sliced mushrooms

½ cup sliced water chestnuts

½ cup sliced bamboo shoots

1 (15-ounce) can baby corn pieces, drained

2 broccoli stalks, florets only, cut into bite-size pieces

¼ cup light teriyaki sauce

3 cups cooked rice

To prepare the leek sauce: Combine the cornstarch and the water in a small bowl and beat with a wire whisk to dissolve; set aside.

Heat ¼ cup peanut oil in a small sauté pan over medium heat. Add the leek, ginger, and cayenne peppers and stir to coat with oil. Sauté for 5 to 7 minutes, or until the leek is golden brown. Add the teriyaki sauce and stir well. Set aside.

To prepare the rice: Heat the second ¼ cup of peanut oil in a large sauté pan or wok. Put the ginger, cayenne peppers, scallions, and garlic in the sauté pan or wok and stir well. Sauté for 3 minutes, stirring often. Add the bean curd and stir well to coat with oil. (It may be necessary to add more oil as you add ingredients.) Sauté for 8 to 10 minutes, stirring often to brown the bean curd on all sides (see Note).

Add the cashews and carrots and stir well. Sauté for 2 minutes, stirring often. Add the celery, mushrooms, water chestnuts, bamboo shoots, and baby corn. Sauté for 5 minutes, stirring often. Add the broccoli, teriyaki sauce, and cooked rice. Stir well and sauté for 7 to 10 minutes, or until the broccoli turns dark green but is still crispy. Keep hot. Restir the dissolved cornstarch mixture and add to the sauce slowly while stirring. Simmer the sauce for about 2 minutes, or until it thickens.

Serve the fried rice with the sauce on the side.

MAKES 6 TO 8 SERVINGS

NOTE: The bean curd may stick to the pan. I tend to analyze cooking problems in the same way that I analyze engine problems. This usu-

ally happens for one of three reasons: First, you may not have drained the tofu sufficiently; second, you may need a bit more oil; and third, the oil may not be hot enough. The sticking is not cause for concern, and one basic technique remedies any cause: Just add a little oil, turn up the heat, scrape the bean curd from the bottom of the pan, and keep sautéing.

Biker Pie

Boy oh boy, this biker does like his pie. In fact, I went ahead and named this one for all the bikers who would die without pie. I have incorporated some of my favorite flavors, things you would not expect to find in a pie. The sun-dried tomatoes mix magically with the cayenne and ancho peppers and are well complemented by the onions and garlic. Add the broccoli and cheese, and it is a little slice of heaven in a flaky crust. Don't die—just run to the kitchen and cook up some pie. Save me a slice, OK?

> 6 sun-dried tomatoes
>
> 1 dried long slim cayenne pepper, stemmed and crushed
>
> 1 ancho pepper, stemmed, seeded, and torn into small pieces
>
> ½ cup boiling water (see page 18)
>
> 1 bunch broccoli
>
> 4 tablespoons (½ stick) margarine
>
> 2 large onions, cut into ½-inch cubes
>
> 2 celery stalks, trimmed and cut into ½-inch slices
>
> 1 tablespoon chopped garlic
>
> ½ teaspoon salt
>
> ½ teaspoon black pepper
>
> 2 cups shredded sharp cheddar cheese
>
> 1 package pie crust mix for a double-crust 9-inch pie

Put the sun-dried tomatoes and cayenne and ancho peppers in a small bowl and cover with boiling water. Set aside and allow to cool to room temperature.

Remove the florets from the broccoli stalks. Break or cut the florets into bite-size pieces and set aside. Trim any leaves or hard dry parts from the broccoli stalks. Cut the stalks into ½-inch slices.

In a large sauté pan, melt the margarine over medium heat. Add the broccoli slices, onions, and celery and sauté for 5 to 7 minutes, or until the stalks start to get tender. Add the broccoli florets and sauté for 3 to

5 minutes, or until the florets start to turn darker green. Remove from heat and allow to cool to room temperature.

Combine the hot pepper mixture with the garlic, salt, and black pepper in a blender or a food processor equipped with a chopping blade. Puree for 1 to 2 minutes, or until smooth and without any solid pieces. You may have to add a little more water to create a thin paste. Add the puree to the cooled vegetables. Stir well to coat all the vegetables with the puree. Add the shredded cheese and toss well.

Preheat the oven to 425°F. (see Note, page 157).

Prepare the pie crusts according to package directions for 1 double-crust 9-inch pie. Put one crust into a 9-inch deep-dish pie pan. Add the vegetables and cheese, then lay the second crust on top. Fold the excess dough under the bottom crust, flute the edge with a fork, and poke several holes in the top crust so the steam can escape while baking.

Bake for 30 minutes, or until the crust is golden brown. Remove the pie from the oven and let cool on a raised pie rack for 10 to 15 minutes. The cooling time allows the cheese to solidify enough to cut the pie into slices that will retain their "slice of pie" shape when served.

MAKES ONE 9-INCH PIE OR 4 TO 6 SERVINGS

Creole Broccoli

When I turn that front tire south, you know I'm searching for some good down-home cooking. But you don't have to ride all the way to Louisiana to enjoy Creole cooking. Just beat a path to the kitchen and cook up this recipe.

 1 bunch broccoli
 4 tablespoons (½ stick) salted butter
 1 fresh long slim red cayenne pepper, stemmed and
     thinly sliced
 1 medium onion, cut into ⅛-inch-thick rings, rings cut
     in half
 1 tablespoon chopped garlic
 1 orange bell pepper, cored, quartered, and julienned
 ½ teaspoon salt
 ½ teaspoon ground black pepper
 2 tablespoons flour
 1 (28-ounce) can whole peeled tomatoes
 2 cups shredded cheddar cheese
 Cooked rice

Preheat the oven to 350°F.

Remove the florets from the broccoli and set aside. Trim and peel the broccoli stalks, then cut into small chunks.

Melt the butter in a large frying pan over medium heat. Add the cayenne pepper, onion, and garlic and sauté for 2 to 3 minutes. Add the broccoli stalks and sauté for 2 to 3 minutes, stirring often. Add the bell pepper and sauté for 2 to 3 minutes, or until the onion is golden brown. Add the salt, black pepper, and flour slowly while stirring, mixing well so there are no lumps of flour.

Transfer the tomatoes from the can to a bowl using a slotted spoon. (Do not drain the tomatoes as you want the juice that is inside them.) Cut the tomatoes into large chunks. Add them to the frying pan with

¼ cup of the tomato juice from the can. Stir well and simmer for 5 minutes.

Break or cut the broccoli florets into bite-size pieces. Add to the frying pan, stir well, and simmer for 5 minutes.

Transfer to a baking dish and cover with the cheddar cheese. Bake for 10 to 15 minutes, or until the cheese is melted and bubbly. Remove from the oven and serve on a bed of rice.

MAKES ABOUT 6 SERVINGS

Hoppin' Bikers

This is my hotheaded biker-style version of a Southern classic, hoppin' John. Legend says that if you eat black-eyed peas on New Year's Day you will have good luck in the upcoming year. Sounds good to me, especially since I love black-eyed peas. The cayenne pepper adds the fire, and the dark beer and Liquid Smoke give this dish a unique flavor. Serve it on New Year's Day or any day you feel the need for a little luck.

6 scallions
2 tablespoons extra-virgin olive oil
1 carrot, peeled and thinly sliced
1 celery stalk, thinly sliced
1 red bell pepper, cored and julienned
1 or more fresh long slim red cayenne peppers, diced
1 (10-ounce) package frozen black-eyed peas, thawed
   and rinsed
1 bay leaf
½ teaspoon salt
½ teaspoon black pepper
1 tablespoon Liquid Smoke
1 tablespoon chopped garlic
1 (12-ounce) bottle dark beer
Cooked rice
1 cup shredded cheddar cheese

Trim the scallions. Remove the dark green tops and set aside. Cut the white and light green sections into ¼-inch-thick slices.

Heat the oil in a large sauté pan over medium heat. Add the carrot and stir well to coat with oil. Add the white and light green sections of the scallions and the celery, reduce the heat to low, and sauté for 2 minutes. Add the bell and cayenne peppers and sauté for about 3 minutes, or until the carrot begins to brown. Add the black-eyed peas and stir well. Sauté for 1 minute.

continued

Add the bay leaf, salt, black pepper, Liquid Smoke, garlic, and beer. Stir well and bring to a boil. Reduce the heat and simmer, covered, for about 10 minutes, or until the liquid is almost completely absorbed— there should still be about $\frac{1}{3}$ cup sauce.

Thinly slice the dark green scallion tops while the mixture simmers. Then stir in half the scallion greens. Ladle the Hoppin' Bikers over a bed of rice and sprinkle some cheese on top. Serve with the remaining scallion greens and cheese on the side.

MAKES ABOUT 4 SERVINGS

Hot Stuffed Hungarian Pancakes

Throughout history, Hungary has been on a trade route from east to west. This has brought many welcome culinary customs and ingredients to Hungary along with hungry Crusaders and invading armies, each cooking and eating everything in sight—sounds like the inspiration for a bad Hollywood biker movie. One result of such a colorful history is that Hungary developed a unique culinary tradition. This recipe will give you a taste of the rich and delicious style of cooking that Hungary is famous for. And if Hollywood movie moguls invade your garage to shoot another bad biker movie, prepare this recipe for them, then, while they are eating, grab their cellular phones and call the reality police.

PANCAKES

  2 tablespoons melted butter
  2 large eggs
  ½ cup half-and-half
  ½ cup plain seltzer
  ⅛ teaspoon salt
  1 teaspoon hot Hungarian paprika
  ½ cup all-purpose flour

continued

Stuffing

1 small green cabbage, quartered, cored, and shredded

1 teaspoon salt

1 teaspoon caraway seeds

6 tablespoons (¾ stick) unsalted butter

1 medium onion, diced

1 fresh long slim red cayenne pepper, stemmed and
   minced

1 teaspoon sugar

1 red bell pepper, cored and julienned

½ cup hot water

2 tablespoons hot Hungarian paprika

1 tablespoon chopped garlic

½ cup sour cream

1 tablespoon flour

Butter, for frying and serving

Sour cream, for serving

To prepare the batter: In a medium mixing bowl, with a wire whisk, beat together the melted butter, eggs, half-and-half, seltzer, salt, and paprika. Add the flour slowly while beating steadily for about 1 minute, or until smooth. Cover tightly and allow to rest for 1 hour in the refrigerator.

To prepare the stuffing: Put the shredded cabbage in a large bowl. Sprinkle with the salt and toss well. Set the cabbage aside for 20 minutes to allow it to shed excess moisture. Drain the cabbage before using.

Heat a medium cast-iron frying pan for about 2 minutes over medium heat. Sprinkle the caraway seeds into the frying pan. Gently shake the frying pan in a circular motion over the heat—this should cause the caraway seeds to gently dance in the pan and toast on all sides without burning. Continue this for 1 to 2 minutes until the first caraway seed pops. Remove the seeds from the pan and set aside.

Melt 2 tablespoons of the butter in the frying pan. Add the onion and sauté until transparent, 2 to 3 minutes. Remove from the heat before the onion begins to brown.

In a large sauté pan, melt 4 more tablespoons of butter over medium

heat. Add the toasted caraway seeds and the cayenne pepper, then sprinkle the sugar into the melted butter. Slowly sauté, stirring until the sugar begins to brown. Add the bell pepper and drained cabbage and stir well to coat with butter. Sauté for about 5 minutes, or until the cabbage begins to look wilted.

In a small bowl, combine the hot water, paprika, and garlic. Add the paprika mixture and onion to the cabbage and stir well. Simmer, covered, for about 20 minutes, stirring every few minutes until the cabbage is tender.

Combine the ½ cup sour cream and the flour. Stir several tablespoons of the hot liquid from the cabbage into the sour cream (this helps prevent curdling), then stir the sour cream mixture into the cabbage. Reduce the heat to very low and simmer until the sauce thickens, about 5 minutes.

To prepare the pancakes: While the sauce is thickening, fry the pancakes. In a medium cast-iron frying pan over moderately high heat, melt enough butter to coat the pan. Pour ¼ cup of batter into the pan and immediately swirl the batter around to form a thin pancake. Fry the pancake for 30 seconds to 1 minute, until the batter is firm and the edges start to brown. (These pancakes are cooked on only one side.) Place the cooked pancake on a plate and keep warm by covering with an inverted plate or a towel. Repeat until all of the pancakes are cooked.

Lay a pancake on a plate, place several spoonfuls of stuffing along one side, and roll the pancake around the stuffing. Drizzle a little melted butter over the rolled pancakes and serve with sour cream on the side.

MAKES 6 TO 8 SERVINGS

Volcano

This recipe is a déjà vu of a high school science fair project gone haywire. Any kid attempting to assemble something that looks like this could count on producing a parental eruption. But the eruptions this dish will produce are amazement at the unique presentation, followed by aftershocks of requests for second servings. Have some friends over for dinner and watch them get blown away by the eruption of spicy beans and cheese from within a mountain of exotic rice and broccoli trees. This one-dish meal will produce an explosion of compliments at your next biker-style dinner party.

Volcano Sauce

2 tablespoons olive oil
2 to 3 chipotle peppers packed in adobo sauce, minced
1 medium onion, minced
2 tablespoons chopped garlic
1 (16-ounce) can dark red kidney beans, rinsed
1 yellow bell pepper, cored and diced
1 (28-ounce) can whole peeled tomatoes, drained and
  coarsely chopped
½ teaspoon salt
½ teaspoon ground black pepper
1 teaspoon dried cilantro

Rice

3 tablespoons margarine
6 small fresh Anaheim peppers, roasted (page 19),
  stemmed, and chopped (about 1 cup)
1 medium onion, diced
2 tablespoons chopped garlic

½ cup cool water

1 teaspoon cumin seeds

1 teaspoon whole black peppercorns

2 cups Texmati® rice

2 teaspoons salt

3½ cups hot water

TO ASSEMBLE:

Vegetable oil spray, for pan preparation

1 fresh habanero pepper, stemmed and seeded

¼ cup Liquid Smoke

4 cups boiling water

1 bunch broccoli

1 cup shredded cheddar cheese

To prepare the sauce: Heat the oil in a large sauté pan over medium heat. Add the chipotle peppers, onion, and garlic and sauté for 3 to 5 minutes, or until the onion is golden. Add the beans, bell pepper, tomatoes, and seasonings. Reduce the heat to low and simmer for about 7 minutes, or until a thick sauce forms. Keep warm while you prepare the rice and broccoli.

To prepare the rice: In a small sauté pan, melt 1 tablespoon of margarine over medium heat. Add the Anaheim peppers, onion, and garlic and sauté for 3 to 5 minutes, or until the onion is golden brown. Add the cool water, remove from the heat, and stir well to deglaze the pan. Transfer to a blender and puree for 1 minute, or until smooth. Set aside.

To assemble the Volcano: Spray the inside of a 10-inch Bundt cake pan with cooking oil spray. (Or use a 3-quart mixing bowl and invert a wide-mouth 8-ounce heatproof glass in the center of the bowl; spray the bowl and glass with cooking oil.) Set aside; this will be the volcano mold.

In a large saucepan, melt the remaining 2 tablespoons of margarine over medium heat. Add the cumin seeds and peppercorns and sauté for about 2 minutes, or until the margarine begins to brown. Add the rice, stir to coat with the margarine, and sauté for about 5 minutes, or until the rice begins to brown. Add the salt, hot water, and reserved pepper

puree and stir well. Bring to a boil, reduce the heat to low, cover, and simmer for 15 to 20 minutes, or until the rice is tender.

Preheat the oven to 350°F.

While the rice is simmering, combine the habanero pepper, Liquid Smoke, and boiling water in a medium saucepan and bring to a simmer over medium heat. Separate the broccoli into florets, each with a piece of stalk about 2 inches long. Put the broccoli into the habanero water and simmer for about 5 minutes, or until the broccoli turns dark green and is tender-crisp; drain and set aside. (The broccoli should be done about the same time the rice is tender.)

Transfer the rice to the prepared Bundt pan or bowl. (If using the bowl, make sure the glass stays centered. Pack the rice firmly so it is level with the glass's bottom.) Place a large pie pan or heatproof serving dish over the bowl and invert. The Bundt pan or mixing bowl should lift off the molded rice. Reshape the sides if necessary, and carefully remove the glass, if used.

Arrange the broccoli florets (discard the habanero) around the base of the mold like trees. Spoon the sauce into the crater to fill the center and run down the sides like lava. Dress with cheese to form "lava flows" and bake for 5 to 10 minutes, or until the cheese melts. Serve immediately.

MAKES 8 SERVINGS

Hot Ceylon Broccoli with Cashews

Have you ever wanted to pack up your scooter and travel around the world in search of spices and adventure? One place you would want to visit is the island of Sri Lanka to try some of their wonderful blending of Indian-style flavors and crispy vegetables reminiscent of Chinese cooking. If you don't have the time to ride halfway around the world to eat lunch at a Sri Lankan restaurant, then just run into your kitchen and prepare this recipe. After dinner you can relax on the sofa with your atlas and plan that dream trip.

1 bunch broccoli

6 scallions

4 tablespoons (½ stick) salted butter

1 fresh long slim red cayenne pepper, stemmed and
  minced

½ cup cashews, coarsely chopped

½ cup shredded unsweetened coconut

1 tablespoon chopped garlic

4 whole cardamom pods, coarsely chopped

1 teaspoon ground cumin

1 teaspoon turmeric

½ teaspoon salt

½ teaspoon ground white pepper

1 red bell pepper, cored and julienned

½ cup hot water

Cooked rice or Hot Krazy Rice (page 211)

Remove the broccoli florets from the stalks. Break or cut the florets into bite-size pieces and set aside. Trim any leaves of hard dry parts from the stalks. Use a food processor equipped with a chopping blade to finely chop the stalks, or mince by hand.

Trim the scallions. Remove the dark green tops and set aside. Cut the white and light green sections into ¼-inch-thick slices.

In a large sauté pan, melt the butter over medium heat. Add the

cayenne pepper and minced broccoli stalks and sauté for 3 to 5 minutes, or until the broccoli stalks begin to brown.

Add the cashews, coconut, garlic, spices, and salt and pepper. Stir well and sauté for 3 to 5 minutes, or until the mixture begins to stick to the pan. Add the white and light green sections of the scallions, the broccoli florets, bell pepper, and water. Stir well to dissolve bits that have stuck to the bottom of the pan. Simmer, covered, for about 5 minutes, stirring often until the broccoli florets turn dark green but are still crispy.

Meanwhile, thinly slice the dark green scallion tops.

Serve hot with plain rice or Hot Krazy Rice, and garnished with the sliced dark green scallion tops.

MAKES 4 TO 6 SERVINGS

Snap Jack Pie

Long rides and country air may leave your soul truly satisfied, but it sure conjures up an awesome appetite. This pie is soul-satisfying with its medley of country-style beans, jack cheese, and smoky chipotle peppers. The flavors will bring that ride-in-the-country feeling right to your table.

> 2 tablespoons butter
> 2 chipotle peppers packed in adobo sauce, minced, sauce reserved
> 6 garlic cloves, thinly sliced
> 1 small onion, quartered and thinly sliced
> 6 scallions
> 1 (9-ounce) package frozen cut green beans, thawed and drained
> 1 (9-ounce) package frozen cut wax beans, thawed and drained
> 1 red bell pepper, cored and cut into pieces the same size as the beans
> 1 teaspoon salt
> ½ teaspoon black pepper
> 1 teaspoon dried cilantro
> ¼ cup boiling water (see page 18)
> 1 package pie crust mix for a double-crust 9-inch pie
> 3 cups shredded Monterey jack cheese

In a large sauté pan, melt the butter over high heat. Add the chipotle, garlic, and onion and sauté for 3 to 5 minutes, or until the onion is golden brown.

While the onion is sautéing, trim the scallions. Remove the dark green tops and set aside. Cut the white and light green sections into ½-inch-thick slices. Add the white and light green sections to the pan along with the green beans, wax beans, and bell pepper. Reduce the heat to medium and sauté for about 3 minutes.

continued

While the beans are sautéing, combine the salt, black pepper, cilantro, 1 teaspoon reserved adobo sauce, and the water in a small bowl. Stir the spice mixture into the beans and simmer for about 2 minutes. Remove from heat and set aside.

Preheat the oven to 350°F. (see Note, page 157).

Prepare the pie crust mix according to package directions for 2 single-crust 9-inch pies. Place the crusts into two 9-inch pie pans and pinch to flute the edges. (This recipe can also be prepared as individual pies by using 6 to 8 medium tart dishes.) Brush the crusts with some additional adobo sauce.

Thinly slice the dark green scallion tops. Add the tops and the cheese to the beans, tossing to combine. Divide the bean mixture between the 2 pie pans. Bake for about 20 minutes, or until the pie crusts are golden brown and the cheese is melted and begins to brown. Allow the pies to cool for a few minutes before slicing; this will help the filling retain its "piece of pie" shape.

MAKES TWO 9-INCH PIES OR 8 TO 12 SERVINGS

Biker Biriyani

This is my revved-up version of a royal Indian dish. All of the ingredients are layered in a large pot, which is then sealed with dough and placed in the oven to roast. This recipe is so delicious you may be crowned "king of the kitchen."

RICE

- 4 cups water
- 2 teaspoons salt
- Generous pinch of saffron
- 2 cups basmati rice, rinsed

VEGETABLES

- 4 tablespoons (½ stick) salted butter
- 1 cup cashews, coarsely chopped
- 1 fresh long slim red cayenne pepper, stemmed
- 2 teaspoons cumin seeds
- 1 teaspoon whole black peppercorns
- 3 cardamom pods
- 1 (3-inch) cinnamon stick
- 1 cup golden raisins
- 1 medium onion, coarsely chopped
- 2 tablespoons chopped garlic
- ½ teaspoon salt
- ½ teaspoon ground coriander
- 1 yellow bell pepper, cored and diced
- 1 red bell pepper, cored and diced
- 2 cups frozen peas and carrots, thawed and drained
- ½ cup shredded unsweetened coconut
- ½ cup hot water

continued

TO ASSEMBLE:

4 tablespoons (½ stick) butter
1 fresh long slim red cayenne pepper
1 tablespoon chopped garlic
1 (3-inch) cinnamon stick
½ teaspoon ground cumin
1 teaspoon turmeric
½ teaspoon ground coriander
½ teaspoon ground black pepper
1 teaspoon salt
½ cup boiling water
2 tablespoons shredded unsweetened coconut

To prepare the rice: In a large saucepan, bring the water to a boil over high heat. Add the salt, saffron, and rice. Stir well, cover tightly, reduce the heat to very low, and simmer for 20 minutes. Do not stir the rice while it cooks; after 20 minutes, remove from the heat and allow to rest. This produces the fluffiest, most firm-textured rice.

To prepare the vegetables: In a large sauté pan, melt 2 tablespoons of the butter over medium heat. Add the cashews and cayenne pepper and sauté for 3 to 5 minutes, or until the cashews are lightly browned. Remove from the heat and use a slotted spoon to transfer the cashews to a small bowl. Keep as much butter as possible in the pan along with the cayenne pepper.

Add the remaining 2 tablespoons butter to the sauté pan and return to medium heat. When the butter has melted, add the cumin seeds, peppercorns, cardamom, and cinnamon stick. Sauté for 2 to 3 minutes, or until the butter is golden. Add the raisins and sauté for 1 minute. Add the onion, garlic, salt, coriander, bell peppers, peas and carrots, and coconut. Toss well and sauté for about 3 minutes, or until the vegetables are almost tender. Reserve ¼ cup of the cashews for garnish and stir the rest into the vegetable mixture. Then add the hot water, stir well to loosen any bits from the bottom of the pan, and cover tightly. Remove from heat and set aside.

To assemble the biriyani: In a wide, deep pot with a tight-fitting cover, melt the butter over medium heat. Add the cayenne pepper, garlic, cin-

namon, cumin, turmeric, coriander, black pepper, and salt. Stir well and sauté for about 3 minutes, or until the butter is golden.

While the spices are cooking, stretch a piece of aluminum foil over the bottom of the pot's lid. When you later place the lid on the pot, the foil should form a seal between the lid and the pot. Add one third of the rice to create a loose layer on the bottom of the pot. On top of that, layer half the vegetables, then add another third of the rice, then the remaining vegetables, and finally the remaining rice. Carefully pour the boiling water in around the edge.

Immediately cover the pot with the foil-lined lid. Make sure it is well sealed. Place over high heat. After 1 minute, reduce the heat to the lowest possible setting and steam for about 5 minutes to infuse the flavors.

Remove the pot from the heat, uncover, and toss the ingredients together with 2 forks. Or, if you can firmly hold the lid on the pot, do it Indian biker–style by shaking the pot up and down several times. Mound onto a large serving platter, remove the whole cayenne peppers, cardamom pods, and cinnamon sticks, and sprinkle with coconut and the reserved cashews. Serve immediately.

MAKES 6 TO 8 SERVINGS

Crepes Happen

There is a biker saying that rhymes with "crepes happen"; in fact, some people wear T-shirts with that expression printed on them. As a biker you learn to accept that life has some unpleasant experiences in it, and all you can do is learn from them and move forward. Well, this recipe can provide a pleasant experience at the end of a long ride, even if it was a rough road.

This recipe has three basic steps. First you prepare the batter. Then, while the batter is resting, you prepare the sauce and the filling. Finally, you fry the crepes and assemble everything. While the crepes take about 1½ hours, they are easy and worth the time. So cook them up, and when everyone raves, you can just say "Hey, crepes happen."

Batter

1 cup all-purpose flour
⅛ teaspoon salt
3 eggs
1½ cups milk
2 tablespoons oil or melted butter

Sauce

1 chipotle pepper packed in adobo sauce, minced
12 sun-dried tomatoes, minced
½ cup boiling water (see page 18)
2 tablespoons salted butter
1 tablespoon chopped garlic
1 medium onion, diced
½ cup cool water
½ cup light cream

FILLING

1 teaspoon dried parsley

1 teaspoon dried cilantro

½ teaspoon salt

½ teaspoon coarsely ground black pepper

½ teaspoon ground coriander

¼ cup boiling water (see page 18)

4 tablespoons salted butter

1 fresh green serrano pepper, stemmed and minced

1 cup baby carrots, halved lengthwise

6 scallions

1 small zucchini, halved lengthwise and cut into ¼-inch
  slices

1 red bell pepper, cored and julienned

1 yellow bell pepper, cored and julienned

1 cup sliced mushrooms

Butter, for frying

To prepare the batter: Combine all the ingredients for the batter in a bowl and mix with a wire whisk until very smooth. (This can also be done in a blender or a food processor equipped with a chopping blade.) Refrigerate for 1 hour in a tightly covered container.

To prepare the sauce: Put the chipotle and sun-dried tomatoes into a small bowl and cover with the boiling water. Set aside and allow to cool to room temperature.

In a small sauté pan, melt the butter over medium heat. Add the garlic and onion and sauté for 3 to 5 minutes, or until the onion is golden. Add the rehydrated chipotle pepper and sun-dried tomatoes, then simmer until all the liquid is absorbed and the mixture begins to fry again, about 2 to 4 minutes. Remove from the heat and add the cool water, stir well to de-glaze the pan, and transfer to a blender or a food processor equipped with a chopping blade. Process for 1 minute, or until there are no large pieces remaining. Add the cream and process until smooth. Return to the small sauté pan and keep warm over very low heat, stirring often to prevent burning or separation.

continued

To prepare the filling: In small bowl, combine the parsley, cilantro, salt, black pepper, and coriander. Cover with the boiling water, set aside, and allow to cool to room temperature.

In a large sauté pan, melt the butter over medium heat. Add the serrano pepper and carrots, stir well to coat with butter, and sauté for 3 to 5 minutes, or until the carrots begin to brown.

While the carrots are sautéing, trim the scallions. Remove the dark green tops and set aside; cut the white and light green sections of the scallions into 1-inch-thick slices. Thinly slice the dark green scallion tops.

Add the white and light green sections of the scallions, the zucchini, bell peppers, and mushrooms to the sauté pan. Sauté for 5 to 7 minutes, or until the vegetables start to become tender but are still firm.

Add the rehydrated spices and water. Reduce the heat to low and simmer until all the liquid is absorbed and the mixture begins to fry again, 2 to 4 minutes. Remove from the heat and keep warm.

To assemble the crepes: In a medium cast-iron frying pan over moderately high heat, melt enough butter to coat the pan. Pour ¼ cup of the batter into the pan and immediately swirl the batter around to form a thin crepe. Fry for 30 seconds to 1 minute, or until the crepe is firm and the edges start to brown. Turn over and fry the other side for 30 seconds to 1 minute. Place the cooked crepe on a plate and keep warm by covering with an inverted plate or a dish towel. Repeat until all the crepes are cooked.

Lay a crepe on a plate, put several spoonfuls of filling in a line down the middle, and fold one side over, then fold the other side over that. Repeat until all the crepes and filling are used up.

Place a few crepes on each plate and pour some sauce over them. Sprinkle with the reserved dark green scallion tops and serve with extra sauce on the side.

MAKES 4 TO 6 SERVINGS

Sidecars: Side Dishes

SIDECARS always attract a lot of attention and seem to almost "tame" the motorcycle they are attached to. People who would look at a motorcycle and rider with suspicion smile and wave at a sidecarist. Everybody wants to ask questions or remembers an ancient family story about an aunt and uncle who rode somewhere in a sidecar. Sidecars are extra cool.

Like sidecars, side dishes help balance the main dish. What constitutes balance on a dinner plate is up to you, but here are some recipes for your culinary balancing act. Pick your third wheel and Cook with Fire.

Masala Potatoes*

One look at this recipe and I knew Carol and David House had a winner. I am always on the lookout for new spices and seasonings to try, and black mustard seeds sounded good to me. Well, I got so excited that I slaughtered the sacred cow of TV cooking show rules—I didn't test the recipe. I just rode to the studio and shot it, making a few changes to the recipe as I cooked it. The rest is biker dinnertime history.

> 3 tablespoons salted butter
> 1 tablespoon black mustard seeds
> 1 fresh long slim red cayenne pepper, stemmed
> ½ teaspoon whole black peppercorns
> 2 medium onions, coarsely chopped
> 1 red bell pepper, cored and diced
> 1 teaspoon turmeric
> ½ teaspoon ground coriander
> ½ teaspoon salt
> 1 to 3 teaspoons ground cayenne pepper
> 4 or 5 medium potatoes, unpeeled, parboiled and cut
>   into 1-inch chunks
> ¼ cup hot water
> Juice of 1 lemon

In a large sauté pan, melt the butter over medium heat. Add the mustard seeds and sauté about 2 minutes, or until the butter begins to brown. Add the whole cayenne pepper, peppercorns, onions, and bell pepper and sauté about 3 minutes, or until the onions are tender.

Add the turmeric, coriander, salt, and ground cayenne. Stir well to blend. Add the potatoes, water, and lemon juice and stir well. Reduce the heat to low and simmer, covered, for 3 to 5 minutes, or until the sauce thickens. Remove the whole cayenne pepper before serving.

MAKES 4 TO 6 SERVINGS

Contest winner

Mexi-Corn

Just try and imagine a world without corn and peppers—the only thing more unbearable would be a world without motorcycles. Well, fear not, there are plenty of corn and peppers and almost enough motorcycles for everyone to enjoy. And this recipe is a good way to enjoy all three. Just take a long ride to the store, buy some corn and peppers, and ride straight to your kitchen. The crisp medley of fresh peppers and sweet corn kernels will complement any meal. And the colorful combination of red, yellow, and green will remind you of traffic lights and the fact that you need to go riding. See, the world is good. Alright!

> 2 tablespoons salted butter
> 1 small red bell pepper, cored and coarsely chopped
> 1 fresh green Anaheim pepper, stemmed and coarsely chopped
> 1 fresh green jalapeño pepper, stemmed and coarsely chopped (optional)
> 1 (12-ounce) can whole kernel corn, drained
> Salt and ground black pepper

In a small saucepan, melt the butter over medium heat. Combine the peppers in the saucepan and simmer for 2 to 3 minutes. Add the corn and stir well. Reduce the heat to low, cover, and simmer for 3 to 5 minutes, stirring often to prevent burning. Season with salt and black pepper to taste and serve piping hot.

MAKES 4 SERVINGS

Hot Garbanzo Beans with
Sun-Dried Tomatoes

I like to ride around and find new roads; I can spend all day just wandering and looking for that special curve or an unexpected vista. One of the beauties of riding is taking the time to explore. I approach cooking in the same way—some days I just open the cabinets and see what I can put together. This simple side dish is one of those unexpected curves in the kitchen. Try it and find a new vista for your tongue.

  2 tablespoons olive oil
  4 sun-dried tomatoes, thinly sliced
  2 garlic cloves, thinly sliced
  ½ medium onion, thinly sliced
  ½ to 1 dried New Mexico pepper, stemmed and crushed
  1 (16-ounce) can garbanzo beans
  Water
  Salt and ground black pepper

Heat the oil in a small sauté pan over medium heat. Add the sun-dried tomatoes, garlic, onion, and New Mexico pepper and sauté for 3 to 5 minutes, or until the onion begins to brown. Add the garbanzo beans and continue to sauté for about 5 minutes, or until the garbanzos begin to brown. Add enough water just to cover the garbanzo beans, then stir well. Reduce the heat to low and simmer for about 5 minutes, or until the liquid is almost gone. Add salt and black pepper to taste and serve immediately.

MAKES 4 SERVINGS

Hot Smoky Potato Latkes

This simple little recipe is very memorable. Everyone I have served it to asks me to cook it again, and there are no leftovers. Jalapeños, onions, garlic, potatoes, and some Liquid Smoke, and you have the start of a Biker Billy Hall of Fame (or Flame) candidate. Like a favorite road you ride time after time, this recipe will bring you pleasure for years to come. So what are you waiting for—me to cook them?

> 2 medium eggs
> Liquid Smoke
> 1 teaspoon salt
> ½ teaspoon ground black pepper
> 2 fresh red jalapeño peppers, stemmed and minced
> 4 garlic cloves, minced
> 2 medium onions, coarsely chopped
> 6 medium red potatoes, shredded
> Stone-ground cornmeal
> Olive or corn oil, for frying
> Cheddar cheese (optional)
> Sour cream
> Applesauce

In a small bowl, combine the eggs, several generous dashes of Liquid Smoke, the salt, and black pepper. Beat the eggs until they are a uniform color, then set aside.

In a large mixing bowl, combine the jalapeños, garlic, onions, and potatoes. Add the egg mixture and toss well to combine. The potatoes and onions will shed some liquid. Add cornmeal a little at a time until the liquid is absorbed and the latke mix is still moist (see Note).

Heat several tablespoons of oil in a frying pan over moderately high heat. Carefully place heaping tablespoons of the latke mix in the frying pan. Fry until golden brown, then turn and brown the other side, about 4 to 8 minutes total. If desired, while the second side is browning, put a

slice of cheddar cheese on each latke. Remove from the oil and drain on paper towels. Serve with sour cream and/or applesauce.

MAKES 12 LATKES OR 4 TO 6 SERVINGS

NOTE: The amount of liquid in the potatoes varies with age and moisture content of the potatoes and onions; therefore the amount of cornmeal needed will be different each time you make this recipe.

Stir-Fried Vegetables

Stir-fried vegetables are an excellent way to add color to any plate. This recipe will also add some fire to your menu. I have used broccoli as the main vegetable, but you can substitute any vegetable you choose. The crispy texture created by stir-frying contrasts well with the smoky oriental seasoning.

    1 bunch broccoli
    2 tablespoons peanut oil
    1 fresh red jalapeño pepper, stemmed and minced
    6 garlic cloves, minced
    3 scallions, cut into ½-inch slices
    1 yellow bell pepper, cored and cut into 1-inch squares
    1 red bell pepper, cored and cut into 1-inch squares
    Ground ginger
    Salt and ground black pepper
    Liquid Smoke
    Light teriyaki sauce

Trim the broccoli, discarding the stalks. Break the florets into bite-size pieces and set aside.

Heat the oil in a large sauté pan or wok over medium heat. Add the jalapeño, garlic, and scallions and stir well to coat with oil. Stir-fry for 1 minute. Add the broccoli florets and bell peppers and stir well to coat with oil. Sprinkle a pinch of ginger, salt, and black pepper over the vegetables. Add several dashes of Liquid Smoke and light teriyaki sauce, then stir well to blend. Stir-fry until the broccoli florets start to turn dark green but are still crispy, 3 to 5 minutes. Adjust the seasonings to suit your taste and serve immediately.

MAKES ABOUT 4 SERVINGS

Stir-Fried Vegetables
with Sun-Dried Tomatoes

This stir-fried vegetable recipe is inspired by the flavors of an Italian garden. The sun-dried tomatoes really come to life when combined with the cayenne peppers. Serve this alongside any pasta dish in the book, or toss it with some pasta to make a salad. One forkful will make you think of summer rides in the country.

> 1 to 2 broccoli stalks
>
> Olive oil
>
> 1 medium onion, quartered and thickly sliced
>
> 5 garlic cloves, thinly sliced
>
> 4 sun-dried tomatoes, thinly sliced
>
> 2 dried long slim cayenne peppers, stemmed and crushed
>
> 1 zucchini, halved lengthwise and cut into ½-inch slices
>
> 1 red bell pepper, cored and cut into ½-inch squares
>
> 1 cup water
>
> Salt and ground black pepper

Trim the broccoli, remove the florets, and break them into bite-size pieces; set aside. Cut the broccoli stalks into irregular chunks, rotating the stalk between cuts and changing the angle of the cut.

Heat the oil in a large sauté pan or wok over high heat. Add the broccoli stalks and stir well to coat with oil. Stir-fry for 2 minutes, or until the broccoli begins to brown. Add the onion, garlic, sun-dried tomatoes, and cayenne peppers and stir-fry until the onion is transparent, 2 to 4 minutes. Add the broccoli florets, zucchini, and bell pepper and stir well to coat with oil. Stir-fry until the onion begins to brown and the broccoli florets turn dark green, 3 to 5 minutes.

continued

Carefully pour in the water, which will generate steam. Stir quickly, cover, and remove from the heat. Let steam for only a few minutes; the vegetables should still be crisp. The water will draw a nice sauce from the sun-dried tomatoes and cayenne peppers. Add salt and black pepper to taste. Serve immediately.

MAKES 4 SERVINGS

Ancho Honey Beans

You don't have to ride to Boston for some righteous all-American beans. They aren't baked and they don't come from Boston, but these are so delicious you may become the hero of your own family's bean revolution.

> 1 ancho pepper, stemmed, seeded, and torn into small pieces
> ¼ cup boiling water (see page 18)
> Peanut oil
> 1 small onion, coarsely chopped
> 4 garlic cloves, coarsely chopped
> 1 red bell pepper, cored and diced
> 1 (16-ounce) can large red kidney beans, rinsed and drained
> 2 to 3 tablespoons honey, or more to taste
> 1 to 2 tablespoons water
> Salt and ground black pepper

Place the ancho pepper in a small bowl and cover with boiling water. Set aside and allow to cool to room temperature. Puree the pepper and water in a blender or a food processor equipped with a chopping blade.

Cover the bottom of a medium frying with peanut oil and place over medium heat. Add the onion and garlic and fry for 3 to 5 minutes, or until the onion is golden brown. Add the ancho puree and stir well. Add the bell pepper and fry for 3 to 5 minutes, or until the pepper is tender. Add the beans to the frying pan and sauté until they begin to brown, about 5 minutes.

Reduce the heat to low and add the honey and water. Adjust the sweetness to taste and stir well. Simmer for 2 to 3 minutes, or until the sauce is thick and bubbly. Add salt and black pepper to taste and serve hot.

MAKES 4 SERVINGS

Spinach Feta Fingers

These just can't be believed—the kind of crunchy concoction bikers dream of. Spinach never had it so good. Imagine: spinach, potatoes, and onion zooming down the culinary highway looking for a good time. Along come some feta cheese, ginger, garlic, cumin, and cayenne pepper. Well, when all these food dudes get cooking, you know it's going to be one hell of a party, and you're the guest of honor. So light a fire and let's roll them spinach feta fingers. Alright!

> 1 large red potato, cut into ¼-inch cubes
>
> 1 large onion
>
> 1 (10-ounce) package frozen chopped spinach, thawed and drained (see Note)
>
> 1 rounded teaspoon ground cumin
>
> 1 level teaspoon ground black pepper
>
> 1 level teaspoon salt
>
> ¼ teaspoon ground ginger
>
> 3 tablespoons chopped garlic
>
> 3 large eggs
>
> 1 (8-ounce) chunk feta cheese, crumbled
>
> 2 fresh long slim red cayenne peppers, stemmed and minced
>
> 2 cups whole wheat flour
>
> 2 cups coarsely ground corn chips
>
> Olive oil, for frying

Place the potato cubes in a saucepan and cover with cool water. Place over medium heat and bring to a boil. Slice the onion into rings, then cut the rings into quarters. Add to the potatoes and simmer until the potatoes are tender, about 5 minutes.

Add the spinach, cumin, black pepper, salt, ginger, and garlic to the pan and stir well. Reduce the heat to low and simmer until the liquid is almost gone, 7 to 10 minutes. Remove from heat and allow to cool to room temperature.

Separate 2 of the eggs, and set the whites aside. Beat the yolks and set aside.

In a large mixing bowl, combine the spinach mixture, feta cheese, cayenne peppers, and egg yolks. Toss together well but don't mash the potatoes. The mix will firm up if you set it in the refrigerator for a while.

In a small bowl, beat the 2 egg whites with the remaining egg.

Place the flour in a wide, shallow bowl. Put the corn chips in another wide, shallow bowl.

Heat $\frac{1}{2}$ inch of olive oil in a large frying pan.

Form "fingers" (about the size of your thumb) of the spinach-feta mix. Roll them in the flour, dip them in the beaten eggs, and roll them in the corn chip crumbs. Fry in the hot oil until golden brown on all sides, 4 to 6 minutes. Drain on paper towels and serve hot.

MAKES 18 TO 24 FINGERS

NOTE: Frozen spinach holds a lot of liquid, so I often find it necessary to press the liquid out when it thaws. If you prefer, use $\frac{1}{2}$ pound of fresh spinach. Fresh spinach should be rinsed, drained, and dried, then chopped into small pieces (do this by hand, as a food processor will overchop).

Hot Tom Potatoes

Potatoes, french fried, baked, or mashed, seem to be a regular part of most dinners. Are you bored yet? Well, this recipe is a different way to jazz up potatoes. They have a bad attitude and they come to the plate with their own ketchup. So get ready for something that is hot and smoky with just a hint of barbecue.

2 fresh long slim red cayenne peppers, stemmed and minced

1 small red onion, coarsely chopped

1 tablespoon Liquid Smoke

2 tablespoons unsulphured molasses

1 teaspoon salt

1 teaspoon ground black pepper

1 tablespoon chopped garlic

½ cup tomato ketchup

1 large baking potato, unpeeled and cut into ¼-inch slices

Yellow cornmeal

Canola or corn oil, for frying

Combine the cayenne peppers, onion, Liquid Smoke, molasses, salt, black pepper, garlic, and ketchup in a blender or food processor equipped with a chopping blade. Puree for 1 to 2 minutes until smooth.

Put the potato slices in a mixing bowl and cover with the sauce, making sure that all the potato slices are coated. Marinate for at least 30 minutes, stirring occasionally.

Preheat the oven to 350°F.

Fill a small, shallow bowl halfway with cornmeal. Have some more cornmeal standing by to sprinkle on the potatoes.

In a small frying pan, heat ½ inch of oil over medium heat.

Stir the potato slices. Making sure that each potato slice is thickly coated with the tomato sauce, lay them one at a time in the cornmeal and sprinkle cornmeal on top. Pick them up with a spatula or fork and place in the hot oil. (You have to handle them with care or the tomato sauce will slide right off the potato slices.) Fry the potatoes a few at a time, in a single layer so they don't stick to each other. Turn them with care, frying both sides until they are golden to deep brown, 3 to 5 minutes total. Remove from the oil and drain on paper towels.

Lay the potato slices on a cookie sheet one layer deep. Bake until they are tender when pierced with a fork, about 10 minutes. Serve piping hot.

MAKES 2 SERVINGS

NOTE: If you increase the recipe to make more servings, use care in increasing the number of cayenne peppers, as the sauce can get very hot real fast.

Wild Stuffed Tomatoes

Wild and exciting, and by no means innocent. Yes, these stuffed tomatoes are guilty of packing wild flavor in an innocent-looking package. The wild rice and the nuts produce a crunchy texture that goes perfectly with the flavors of the ancho and pasilla peppers. So bake them up and put a wild one on your plate.

2 cups water

1½ teaspoons salt

4 ounces wild rice (about ¾ cup)

1 ancho pepper, stemmed, seeded, and torn into small
     pieces

1 pasilla pepper, stemmed, seeded, and torn into small
     pieces

1 teaspoon dried cilantro

1 teaspoon dried parsley

½ cup boiling water (see page 18)

4 tablespoons (½ stick) salted butter

1 medium onion, coarsely chopped

1 tablespoon chopped garlic

1 red bell pepper, cored and diced

1 teaspoon ground black pepper

½ cup roasted cashews, coarsely chopped

½ cup roasted peanuts, coarsely chopped

½ cup hot water

4 large tomatoes

SAUCE

2 tablespoons extra-virgin olive oil

1 small onion, coarsely chopped

1 tablespoon chopped garlic

1 fresh long slim red cayenne pepper, stemmed and
   minced
½ teaspoon salt
½ teaspoon black pepper
½ teaspoon ground cumin
2 tablespoons paprika
1 cup shredded cheddar cheese

In a small saucepan, bring the water and ½ teaspoon salt to a boil. Stir in the wild rice, reduce the heat to low, and simmer, covered, for about 50 minutes. Remove from the heat and allow the rice to rest, covered, to absorb the remaining liquid. (If the rice package instructions are different, prepare accordingly.)

In a small bowl, combine the ancho and pasilla peppers, cilantro, and parsley. Cover with boiling water and set aside.

Melt the butter in a large sauté pan over medium heat. Add the onion, garlic, bell pepper, remaining teaspoon of salt, and black pepper. Stir well to coat. Grab the nuts one handful at a time, hold over the sauté pan, and crush them into the pan with your fist while yelling, "Alright!" Sauté for 3 to 5 minutes, or until the onion is golden brown.

Puree the hot pepper mixture in a blender for 1 minute, or until smooth, then add to the sauté pan. Reduce the heat to low and simmer for 3 to 5 minutes, or until the liquid is gone and the mixture begins to stick to the pan. Add the hot water and the cooked wild rice. Stir well, then simmer for about 5 minutes, or until the liquid has been absorbed. Remove from heat.

Preheat the oven to 350°F.

Working over a bowl to catch the flesh and juices, gently remove a ¼-inch-slice from the stem end of each tomato. Use a spoon to scrape out the center, being careful not to break the outer wall of flesh and skin. Set the tomato tops and centers aside. Place the hollow tomato shells upside down on a plate and allow to drain. Coarsely chop the tomato tops and centers.

Heat the oil for the sauce in a small sauté pan over medium heat. Add the onion, garlic, and cayenne pepper and sauté for 3 to 5 minutes, or until the onion is golden brown. Add the salt, black pepper, cumin, paprika, and chopped tomatoes. Bring to a boil, reduce the heat, and simmer for 5 to 10 minutes, or until the sauce thickens.

continued

Stuff the tomatoes with some of the wild rice mixture. Use the excess to form a layer on the bottom of a 9- × 12-inch rectangular baking dish. Place the stuffed tomatoes in the baking dish with the layer of wild rice stuffing as support to keep the tomatoes level. Cover each tomato with cheese and bake for about 40 minutes, or until the tomato shells are tender and the cheese is browned. Serve warm with some of the extra rice and with the sauce on the side.

MAKES 4 STUFFED TOMATOES

Stuffed Acorn Squash

Acorn squash is a wonderful winter vegetable that always reminds me of happy holiday dinners. This recipe is a favorite treat at my house all winter long. I combine hot and sweet to produce a tasty adventure for your tongue. The dried fruit and cashews add to the festive feel of this dish, and make it at home on a Thanksgiving table. But you don't need a holiday to celebrate with this dish. Anytime is good.

> 2 tablespoons honey
> ¼ cup golden molasses
> 4 tablespoons (½ stick) salted butter, softened
> 1 fresh long slim red cayenne pepper, stemmed and
>   minced
> ¼ cup roasted cashews, coarsely chopped
> 4 dates, pitted and minced
> ¼ cup golden raisins
> 2 acorn squashes, halved and seeded
> 2 tablespoons melted butter or margarine

Preheat the oven to 350°F.

Combine the honey, molasses, and 4 tablespoons butter in a food processor. Process with the chopping blade for 1 minute, or until the butter is completely blended with the honey and molasses. Add the cayenne pepper, cashews, dates, and raisins and pulse several times, until the fruits and nuts are fully incorporated. (To prepare this by hand, put the honey, molasses, and butter in a medium mixing bowl, place that bowl in a larger bowl that is one quarter filled with hot tap water. Allow the smaller bowl to sit in the hot water for 2 to 4 minutes. Remove the bowl from the hot water and whip the honey, molasses, and butter with a wire whisk until smooth. Immediately add the cayenne pepper, cashews, dates, and raisins, then whip again until the fruits and nuts are fully incorporated into the honey mixture.)

Slice a small piece from the bottom of each acorn squash half to allow them to sit level in the baking dish. Divide the stuffing mixture evenly

among the 4 acorn squash halves. Brush the bottom of a large baking dish with the melted butter. Arrange the 4 stuffed acorn squash halves in the dish and brush the tops with butter. Bake for 1 hour. Every 15 minutes, brush more butter on the tops of the squash. The squash is done when it can be easily pierced with a fork halfway up the side.

MAKES 4 SERVINGS

Hot Nutty Butternut Squash

This is another winter squash winner. The butternut squash works well with the peanut butter and cashews, creating an unexpected treat. If you like the combo of nuts and fire, then you'll go nuts for this one. You can slice the baked squash or scoop it out of the skin and mash it like potatoes with the filling. Baked potatoes move over or get squashed!

4 tablespoons (½ stick) salted butter

1 fresh red serrano pepper, stemmed and minced

½ cup cashews, coarsely chopped

½ cup currants

½ cup chunky peanut butter

1 tablespoon dark brown sugar, packed

1 butternut squash, halved lengthwise and seeded

Preheat the oven to 400°F.

Melt the butter in a small sauté pan over low heat. Add the serrano pepper and cashews and sauté for 5 minutes, stirring often. Add the currants and sauté for 2 minutes. Add the peanut butter and stir until melted, then add the brown sugar. Stir well and remove from the heat.

A butternut squash has a cavity at the blossom end and a long solid section that extends to the stem. Using a paring knife, make several ¼-inch-deep cuts in the flesh extending from the cavity to the stem end. Place the squash halves in a baking dish and cover the cut surface with the nut mixture. Divide the remaining nut mixture between the two cavities. Bake for 60 to 70 minutes, or until a fork can be easily inserted through the skin into the solid section of squash.

MAKES ABOUT 6 SERVINGS

Batter-Dipped Squash Fries

These are fun to serve, and they are so tasty that they surprise people. Squash is not famous for being exciting, but these will excite your palate and the plate will be empty before you know what happened. Give the french fries a vacation and serve these. You may just have to ride back to the store for another load of squash.

> 1 fresh habanero pepper, stemmed and seeded
> 1 tablespoon chopped garlic
> 1 tablespoon salt
> 1 cup water, or more as needed
> 1 butternut squash, peeled and seeded, cut into
>   strips 2 inches long and ½ inch thick

BATTER

> 1 cup complete biscuit mix, such as Bisquick
> 1 teaspoon crushed red pepper
> 1 teaspoon salt
> ½ teaspoon black pepper
> ¾ cup beer, or more as needed
>
> Oil, for frying

In a blender, puree the habanero pepper, garlic, salt, and water.

Put the squash "fries" in a large saucepan. Add the habanero puree and enough additional water to cover the squash. Bring the water to a boil over high heat. Remove from the heat and allow to cool to room temperature. Drain and set aside.

In a medium mixing bowl, combine the biscuit mix, red pepper, salt, and black pepper. Add the beer and beat with a wire whisk. The batter should be just a little thinner than pancake batter; to achieve this consistency you may need to add more beer a tablespoon at a time.

Heat several inches of oil in a deep pot or a deep-fryer.

Dip the squash fries in the batter and fry a few at a time in the hot oil. Don't put too many in at once because the oil temperature will drop too much and the batter will not fry properly. Fry each batch for 3 to 5 minutes, or until golden brown. Drain on paper towels and serve piping hot.

MAKES 4 TO 6 SERVINGS

Squash Latkes

I like latkes, those wonderful potato pancakes. But I can never leave well enough alone. Since I also love squash, what could be more fun than to combine the two? The choice of squash is up to you—I have used all the winter varieties with this recipe. Each is a little different, and they are all different from potatoes. Go ahead and experiment. I have fun trying new things in the kitchen and you will, too.

3 large eggs

1 fresh long slim red cayenne pepper, stemmed and minced

1 teaspoon salt

1 teaspoon ground black pepper

2 cups peeled, seeded, and shredded winter squash

1 medium onion, minced

¼ cup stone-ground cornmeal

Oil, for frying

In a small mixing bowl, beat together the eggs, cayenne pepper, salt, and black pepper.

In a large mixing bowl, combine the squash and onion. Add the cornmeal and toss well. Then add the egg mixture and toss to completely combine.

Heat several tablespoons of oil in a medium frying pan. Place the latke mix by heaping tablespoons into the oil and flatten gently with the back of the spoon, forming thick patties. Fry for 2 to 3 minutes, or until the edges start to brown. Turn and fry the other side for another 2 to 3 minutes. The latkes should be golden brown on the outside and moist and tender on the inside. Drain on paper towels and serve piping hot.

MAKES 4 SERVINGS

Hot Krazy Rice

This Sri Lankan–inspired rice dish is tasty enough to make any meal an adventure. The flavors are unique but subtle, fire blending with the richness of the coconut milk and punctuated by the sweetness of raisins. It is truly fit for a royal palate and will complement any of the Eastern-style dishes in this book. Try it and you'll go Krazy.

2 tablespoons salted butter
1 fresh long slim red cayenne pepper, stemmed and
    minced
1 medium onion, minced
½ cup golden raisins
1 teaspoon salt
½ teaspoon ground white pepper
½ teaspoon turmeric
½ teaspoon ground cloves
½ teaspoon ground coriander
1 cup Texmati® rice
1 tablespoon honey
1 cup coconut milk
1 cup water

In a large sauté pan, melt the butter over medium heat. Add the cayenne and onion and sauté for 2 to 3 minutes, or until the onion is transparent. Add the raisins and seasonings, stirring well to dissolve the spices. Sauté for 2 to 3 minutes, or until the butter is golden.

Stir in the rice and sauté while stirring constantly for 1 minute. Add the honey, coconut milk, and water. Stir well and bring to a boil, reduce the heat to the lowest possible setting, and simmer, covered, for 15 minutes. Fluff with a fork and serve.

MAKES 4 SERVINGS

Stuart's Zucchini Fritters*

This winning contest entry was sent in by Stuart L. Linder, who based his recipe on my Hot Smoky Potato Latkes (page 192). These zucchini fritters are great with Mulligatawny My Way (page 112) for a light lunch after a morning of motorcycle maintenance. You might just reach a state of biker zen.

> 2 dried New Mexico peppers, stemmed, seeded, and torn
>   into small pieces
> ¼ cup boiling water (see page 18)
> 2 large eggs
> 1 teaspoon salt
> 1 teaspoon ground black pepper
> 1 teaspoon ground cumin
> 1 tablespoon chopped garlic
> 1 cup all-purpose flour
> ½ teaspoon baking powder
> 4 small zucchini, shredded
> 1 medium onion, coarsely chopped
> Olive oil, for frying

Place the New Mexico peppers in a small bowl and cover with boiling water. Set aside and allow to rehydrate for 5 to 10 minutes.

Put the rehydrated peppers and water in a blender or food processor equipped with a chopping blade. Puree for 1 to 2 minutes, or until smooth, then add the eggs, salt, black pepper, cumin, garlic, ½ cup of the flour, and the baking powder. Puree again for 30 seconds to 1 minute, or until the batter is smooth.

Combine the batter with the shredded zucchini, the onion, and the remaining ½ cup flour in a large mixing bowl.

To prepare the fritters: In a medium frying pan, heat ½ inch of olive oil over medium heat.

Place a tablespoon of the zucchini mixture into the oil and flatten gently with the back of a spoon. Repeat until the pan is full of fritters. Fry for 2 to 3 minutes, or until the edges start to brown. Turn and fry the other side for another 2 to 3 minutes. Drain on paper towels and serve piping hot.

MAKES 4 SERVINGS

Contest winner

Biker Breads

I TEND to think a meal is incomplete without some sort of bread—and I'm not talking about the soft, white stuff most of us grew up on. The breads in this section run the gamut from pepper-studded corn-bread to ancho tortillas. From baked loaves to fried and even boiled, all the breads have one thing in common—they all contain fire so they can help you transcend the "white bread syndrome." Alright!

Drop-Dead Cornbread

One of the great pleasures of motorcycle touring in the South is cornbread. Almost every place you stop to eat at will have some fresh, delicious cornbread just waiting to melt in your mouth. Well, I've taken a down-home favorite and pumped it up with some high-octane fire, Southern biker–style. So ride out and get yourself some good stone-ground yellow cornmeal, 'cause that's one of the secrets to achieving great taste and texture. Then heat up grandma's cast-iron skillet, cause cast iron will bake that bread just right. And when you taste that first warm piece of cornbread, you'll holler "Alright!"

> 5 tablespoons butter
> 2 fresh long slim red cayenne peppers, stemmed and
>   minced
> 2 medium onions, minced
> 1 cup stone-ground yellow cornmeal
> 1 cup all-purpose flour
> 3 tablespoons baking powder
> 1 teaspoon salt
> 1 jumbo egg
> 2 tablespoons honey
> 2 tablespoons golden molasses
> 1 cup milk
> Corn oil

Preheat the oven to 425°F.

Melt the butter in a 9-inch heavy cast-iron frying pan over medium heat. Add the cayenne peppers and onions and gently cook 2 to 4 minutes, or until the onions are tender. You do not want to "fry" the onions or darken them. Remove from heat and allow to cool.

In a large mixing bowl, combine the cornmeal, flour, baking powder, and salt. Using a dough cutter, cut the onion and pepper mixture into the dry ingredients. At this point you should make sure that all the cornmeal is "buttered."

In a small mixing bowl, beat the egg. Add the honey, molasses, and milk and blend thoroughly. Add the liquid ingredients to the dry mix. Stir just enough to combine the wet with the dry; don't overmix or you will ruin the texture of the finished cornbread.

Use corn oil to generously grease the cast-iron frying pan you cooked the onions in. Place it in the oven until it is hot.

Carefully remove the frying pan from the oven. Make sure that the pan is completely greased and pour off the excess oil. Pour the cornbread mix into the hot pan. The batter should sizzle when it hits the surface. Return to the oven and bake for 25 to 30 minutes, or until golden brown.

MAKES ONE 9-INCH LOAF

NOTE: You can also cook this cornbread batter as patties in a skillet to make hot johnnycakes.

Howlin' Hush Puppies

You'll howl with delight as you eat these bite-size deep-fried bullets of flavor. These down-home cornbread treats are good as munchies or as a zesty replacement for bread. You can dip them in the Howlin' Cheese Dip (page 54) or Chile con Queso (page 53). I remember enjoying hush puppies as a child on trips down South, but those were tame by comparison. These little devils are straight from the wild side!

> 1 cup stone-ground cornmeal
> 1 teaspoon baking powder
> ½ teaspoon salt
> 1 fresh red or green jalapeño pepper, stemmed and
>   minced
> 1 small onion, minced
> 1 extra-large egg, beaten
> ½ cup half-and-half or milk
> Peanut oil, for frying

Combine the dry ingredients in a large mixing bowl. Add the jalapeño pepper and onion and mix.

In a small mixing bowl, beat the egg and milk. Add to the cornmeal mix, stirring just enough to wet the dry ingredients. Don't overmix, or the texture will be damaged.

Heat several inches of oil in a deep-fryer or 1-quart saucepan.

Use a teaspoon to place a small scoop of mix into the hot oil. You want bite-size hush puppies. Don't put too many in the oil at once or the oil temperature will drop too much. This will reduce the crispness and allow the hush puppies to absorb more oil. Fry until they are golden to deep brown, 2 to 4 minutes. Drain on paper towels and serve immediately.

MAKES 24 TO 36 HUSH PUPPIES

Mammaw's Yam Bread

When I was growing up, I called my grandmother, who lived in Tennessee, Mammaw. This recipe reminds me of the delicious home-cooked food she prepared on her wood stove. Mammaw had a truck farm where she grew a lot of her own food. Her kitchen was the gathering place and focus of much family activity. I hope the aroma of this bread as it bakes will remind you of happy times, too.

> 2 fresh long slim red cayenne peppers, stemmed and
>   minced
> 7 tablespoons butter, softened
> ¼ cup dark molasses
> ¼ cup honey
> 2 extra-large eggs
> ⅓ cup half-and-half
> 1 cup mashed cooked yams (see Note)
> ¾ cup unbleached all-purpose flour
> ½ teaspoon baking powder
> ½ teaspoon baking soda
> ½ teaspoon salt
> ½ teaspoon ground cinnamon
> ½ teaspoon ground nutmeg

In a blender or food processor equipped with a chopping blade, combine the cayenne peppers, 6 tablespoons of the butter, the molasses, honey, eggs, and half-and-half. Process for 1 to 2 minutes, or until thoroughly blended. You want to liquefy the hot peppers. Add the yams and process until pureed.

In a large bowl, combine the flour, baking powder, baking soda, salt, cinnamon, and nutmeg.

Preheat the oven to 350°F.

Put the remaining tablespoon of butter in a 9-inch heavy cast-iron frying pan and place the pan in the oven. When the butter melts, swirl it around to fully coat the pan.

continued

Add the yam mixture to the dry ingredients. Blend just enough to fully combine; don't overmix. Pour the batter into the hot frying pan, return to the oven, and bake for 30 minutes, or until a knife inserted into the center comes out clean.

MAKES ONE 9-INCH LOAF

NOTE: To cook yams, peel, quarter, and cut them into 1-inch chunks. Place in a large saucepan, cover with water, bring to a boil, and cook until tender, 15 to 20 minutes.

Stuffing

Ah, the pleasures of a vast holiday table groaning under the weight of everything the harvest brings. Hidden among all those goodies is the most sought-after prize, the stuffing. Well, there is no point in hiding this high-powered stuffing—it can stand proudly next to any dish. This stuffing is all fired up and ready to roar. In a bird or all by itself, it will take your taste buds for a fast ride to happiness.

½ cup (1 stick) salted butter or margarine

2 medium onions, coarsely diced

2 fresh long slim red cayenne peppers, stemmed and minced

2 tablespoons chopped garlic

1 cup roasted cashews, coarsely chopped

2 tablespoons dried parsley

1 teaspoon salt

1 teaspoon black pepper

1 teaspoon ground paprika

1 cup water

4 cups (8 ounces) unseasoned stuffing mix or toasted bread cut into ¼-inch cubes

2 tablespoons melted butter or margarine

Preheat the oven to 350°F.

Melt the butter in a large saucepan over medium heat. Add the onions, cayenne peppers, garlic, and cashews and stir well. Sauté for 2 to 3 minutes, or until the onions become transparent. It is not necessary to brown the onions.

Add the parsley, salt, black pepper, paprika, and water. Bring to a boil, stirring well to blend the spices. Add the stuffing mix and toss until all the liquid has been absorbed by the bread cubes.

Place the stuffing in a baking dish (see Note) and shape it into a loaf. Brush with melted butter and bake for 20 to 40 minutes, or until the

stuffing is golden brown. The stuffing should be crisp on the outside but still moist and tender on the inside.

MAKES ABOUT 8 SERVINGS

NOTE: For a crispy stuffing use a 9-inch pie pan. For a moister stuffing use a 9-inch loaf pan and cover with aluminum foil for half the baking time.

Jalapeño and Cheese-Stuffed Beer Biscuits

If you like *chiles rellenos* but want to have a little room for the main course, try these tasty, biker-size morsels.

> **6 fresh red or pickled jalapeño peppers, cored**
> **6 ounces cheddar cheese**
> **1 cup complete biscuit mix, such as Bisquick**
> **¼ to ½ cup beer**
> **Butter or vegetable oil spray**

Slice each pepper open from stem end to tip. If you are using pickled jalapeños, rinse off excess vinegar or blot with paper towels. Cut the cheese into 6 pieces sized to fit inside the jalapeños.

In a medium mixing bowl, combine the biscuit mix and beer. (Read the package instructions for rolled biscuits and adjust the measurements as needed.) Form the dough into a ball, then roll it out on a floured surface with a floured rolling pin. You want to form a rectangle that you can cut into 6 squares, each large enough to wrap around one of the cheese-stuffed jalapeño peppers.

Preheat the oven to 450°F. (again check the biscuit mix package for recommendations). Grease a 6-cup muffin pan with the butter or vegetable oil spray.

Put a piece of cheese inside each jalapeño. Place the peppers on the dough squares and fold the corners together over the jalapeños. Place in the muffin pan with the folded side down.

Bake for 7 to 10 minutes, or until the biscuits are golden brown (again, check your package for recommendations).

MAKES 6 BISCUITS

Ancho Tortillas

Fresh homemade tortillas are a biker's delight. I've customized this recipe by adding an ancho pepper. The key to making tortillas is in the preparation and practice. You'll need several sheets of waxed paper, a rolling pin (or tortilla press), and a well-seasoned heavy cast-iron frying pan. Have a towel-lined basket or bowl standing by to keep the tortillas warm and moist.

> 1 ancho pepper, stemmed, seeded, and torn into small
>   pieces
> 1¼ cups boiling water (see page 18)
> 2 cups masa harina (see Note)

Put the ancho pepper in a small bowl and cover with the boiling water. Set aside and allow to cool to room temperature.

Puree the ancho and water in a blender for 1 minute, or until there are no large pieces of pepper remaining.

Put the masa harina in a large mixing bowl and add the pepper puree. Mix with a dough cutter or fork. When a dough forms, remove it from the bowl and knead with your hands for 2 to 3 minutes. The dough should be a little dry but not crumbly. (Test the dough by proceeding with the next step. If the dough is too dry, it will fall apart when you try to form it. If it is too wet and sticky, the waxed paper will not peel away easily.) Adjust by adding a little water or masa harina and rekneading the dough.

Form the dough into 1-inch balls one at a time and flatten into a disk between your palms. Place each disk between two pieces of waxed paper and roll with a rolling pin. Roll from the center out to the edge, rotating the tortilla one quarter turn between each roll until the tortilla is ⅛ inch thick and approximately 8 inches in diameter. (If you are using a tortilla press, follow the manufacturer's instructions.) Carefully peel away one piece of waxed paper, lay the exposed tortilla on the palm of your hand, and gently peel away the other piece of waxed paper, taking care not to tear the tortilla.

Heat a large well-seasoned heavy cast-iron frying pan over moderately high heat. Do not add any oil. The pan is hot enough when a drop of water dances and evaporates rapidly, but the pan should not be smoking.

Prepare one tortilla at a time. (While each tortilla is frying, you should form and roll the next one. This ensures the moistest finished tortillas.) Lay the rolled tortilla in the hot pan. When the edges begin to curl, turn the tortilla over and cook for 30 seconds to 1 minute more. The finished tortilla should be lightly browned in places but flexible. Remove from the pan and place in the prepared basket, covering immediately with the towel.

MAKES 12 TO 18 TORTILLAS

NOTE: Masa harina is a form of cornmeal that can be found in Latin markets if your local supermarket does not stock it. Masa harina is finer than stone-ground cornmeal and produces a delicious tortilla that is nothing like the packaged coarse yellow corn tortillas most supermarkets sell.

Hot Flour Empanada Dough

Try this with Mexican Biker Turnovers (page 38). Or be creative—wrap any of your favorite foods (precooked) in this dough and deep-fry biker-style.

> 1 ancho pepper, stemmed, seeded, and torn into small
>   pieces
> 1 pasilla pepper, stemmed, seeded, and torn into small
>   pieces
> ¼ cup boiling water (see page 18)
> 4 tablespoons (½ stick) salted butter, softened
> 1½ teaspoons salt
> 2 cups all-purpose flour, plus extra for kneading
> 2 large eggs, beaten

Place the ancho and pasilla peppers in a small bowl and cover with the boiling water. Set aside and allow to rehydrate for about 15 minutes.

Hand method: Puree the pepper mixture and butter in a blender. In a large bowl, combine the salt and flour. Cut the pepper puree into the flour using a dough cutter or 2 knifes. Add the beaten eggs and mix with a dough cutter or a fork. When a dough has formed, remove it from the bowl and knead on a floured board for 2 to 3 minutes. The dough should not be sticky; if it is, work in a little extra flour as you knead until it is no longer sticky. Place the dough in a covered bowl or zippered plastic bag and let rest for 30 minutes while you prepare the filling.

Food processor method: Puree the pepper mixture, butter, and salt in a food processor equipped with a chopping blade. Add the flour 1 cup at a time, processing for about 1 minute with each addition until the pepper mixture is well cut into the flour. Slowly add the eggs through the feed tube while processing. Continue to process until the dough forms a ball that revolves around the processor bowl. It may be necessary to stop processing after all the eggs have been added to scrape down the sides of the bowl. If the dough sticks to the processor bowl, add a little flour and process again. The dough should not be sticky and should

freely separate from the food processor bowl and blade. Place the dough in a covered bowl or a zippered plastic bag and let rest for 30 minutes while you prepare the filling.

Form the dough into 1-inch balls one at a time and flatten into a disk between your palms. Place each disk between two pieces of lightly floured waxed paper and roll with a rolling pin. Roll from the center out to the edge, rotating the dough one quarter turn between each roll until the dough is ¼ inch thick and approximately 4 inches in diameter. Carefully peel away one piece of waxed paper, lay the exposed dough on the palm of your hand, and gently peel away the other piece of waxed paper, taking care not to tear the dough.

MAKES 12 TO 18 EMPANADAS

Hot Corn Empanada Dough

This tasty corn-based dough is made with masa harina (see Note, page 225), which produces a crispier crust than wheat flour. The dough is not as flexible as the flour version, so use a little more care (and less filling) when forming the empanadas. Try this with Mexican Biker Turnovers, page 38.

> 1 ancho pepper, stemmed, seeded, and torn into small
>   pieces
> 1 pasilla pepper, stemmed, seeded, and torn into small
>   pieces
> ¼ cup boiling water (see page 18)
> 1⅛ cups cool water
> 2 cups masa harina, plus extra, if necessary, for kneading

Place the ancho and pasilla peppers in a small bowl and cover with the boiling water. Set aside and allow to rehydrate for about 15 minutes.

Hand method: Puree the pepper mixture and the cool water in a blender. Put the masa harina in a large mixing bowl and add the pepper puree. Mix with a dough cutter or fork. When a dough forms, remove it from the bowl and knead with your hands for 2 to 3 minutes. The dough should be a little dry but not crumbly. (Test the dough by proceeding with the next step. If the dough is too dry, it will fall apart when you try to form it. If it is too wet and sticky, the waxed paper will not peel away easily.) Adjust by adding a little water or masa harina and rekneading the dough. Place the dough in a covered bowl or a zippered plastic bag and let it rest for 30 minutes while you prepare the filling.

Food processor method: Puree the pepper mixture and the cool water in a food processor equipped with a chopping blade. Add the masa harina and process until the dough forms a ball that revolves around the processor bowl. It may be necessary to stop processing once or twice to scrape down the sides of the bowl. If the dough sticks to the processor bowl, add a little masa harina and process again. The dough should not be sticky and should freely separate from the food processor bowl and blade. (Test the dough by proceeding with the next step. If the dough is too dry, it will fall apart when you try to form it. If it is too wet and sticky, the waxed paper will not peel away easily.) Adjust by adding a little water or masa harina and processing the dough. Place the dough in a covered bowl or a zippered plastic bag and let it rest for 30 minutes while you prepare the filling.

Form the dough into 1-inch balls one at a time and flatten into a disk between your palms. Place each disk between two pieces of waxed paper and roll with a rolling pin. Roll from the center out to the edge, rotating the dough one quarter turn between each roll until the dough is $\frac{1}{4}$ inch thick and approximately 4 inches in diameter. Carefully peel away one piece of waxed paper, lay the exposed dough on the palm of your hand, and gently peel away the other piece of waxed paper, taking care not to tear the dough.

MAKES 12 TO 18 EMPANADAS

Cornmeal Dumplings

Sometimes a soup will call out for something to give it a little extra stamina. Crackers or croutons may be too wimpy. If you are seeking an accompaniment that will pack a punch and give you something to sink your teeth into, try these dumplings—your soup will never be the same again.

STOCK

2 dried New Mexico peppers
2 dried long slim cayenne peppers
1 tablespoon ground white pepper
2 tablespoons chopped garlic
1 medium onion, coarsely chopped
6 cups water

DUMPLINGS

1 cup cornmeal
½ teaspoon salt
¼ teaspoon ground white pepper
1 tablespoon butter
½ cup boiling water

In a large pot, combine the New Mexico and cayenne peppers, white pepper, garlic, onion, and water. Bring to a boil, reduce the heat, and simmer about 15 minutes, or until the peppers have settled to the bottom. While the stock simmers, prepare the dumplings.

In a medium mixing bowl, combine the cornmeal, salt, and white pepper.

In a small bowl, allow the butter to melt in the boiling water. Add the buttered water to the cornmeal. Blend with a fork until a dough forms.

As soon as the dough has cooled enough to be handled comfortably, form it into $\frac{1}{2}$-inch balls. Flatten the balls a little between your palms; they should look like mini hockey pucks.

Place the dumplings a few at a time in the simmering stock. Simmer for 5 to 10 minutes, or until the dumplings float. Serve the dumplings in your favorite soup, such as Mean Black Bean Soup (page 108).

MAKES ABOUT 20 DUMPLINGS

The Ride's End: Desserts

THE ROAD flows ever onward, always asking you to ride just a few more miles. But sooner or later you turn that big wheel toward home and the end of another wonderful ride, and home is so much nicer after being away. A good meal can have the same powerful attraction, but you want to leave a little room for dessert. After a fiery meal, what can you have for dessert that will complete the experience? If you have had enough fire for the day, try some ice cream to cool off. But if you are like me and you hear the call of fire and want more, then you are ready. For it is in the contrast of sweet and fire that you can truly find fulfillment in any meal. Try some of these desserts—they are hot and sweet and oh-so-good to eat.

Biker Yam Pie

This is one of my favorite desserts, but it is so full flavored and un-dessertlike that it also makes a great lunch dish. I often pack a slice in my saddlebag when I'm going out for a Sunday ride, but even then I like to leave it for last—it's that good. The flavors give me that down-home country feeling I get from riding to grandma's house, and of course the flling has that biker kick to it. So grab your slice of the pie before it's all gone.

> 1 fresh habanero pepper, stemmed, seeded, and minced
>
> ⅓ cup chunky peanut butter
>
> 2 tablespoons golden molasses
>
> ¼ cup honey
>
> 1 extra-large egg
>
> 1 cup half-and-half
>
> ½ teaspoon ground cinnamon
>
> ½ teaspoon ground nutmeg
>
> ¼ teaspoon ground cloves
>
> ½ teaspoon ground ginger
>
> 1 teaspoon vanilla extract
>
> 1 package pie crust mix for a double-crust 9-inch pie
>
> 2 packed cups cooked yams (see Note, page 220)

Preheat the oven to 400°F. (see Note, page 157).

In a blender or a food processor equipped with a chopping blade, combine the habanero pepper, peanut butter, molasses, honey, and egg. Process for 1 to 2 minutes, or until thoroughly blended. Add the half-and-half, cinnamon, nutmeg, cloves, ginger, and vanilla. Process for 1 to 2 minutes, or until thoroughly blended.

Prepare the pie crust according to package directions; however, roll out the whole mixture as one double-thick crust. Place the crust in a 9-inch deep-dish pie pan and pinch to flute the edge.

In a large mixing bowl, mash the yams by hand with a potato masher. Add the puree to the mashed yams and blend until just smooth.

Pour the filling into the pie crust and bake for 45 to 60 minutes, or until a knife inserted into the center of the pie comes out clean.

MAKES ONE 9-INCH PIE OR 4 TO 6 SERVINGS

Gingerbread Bikers from Hell

Do you think of gingerbread cookies as those flavorless things given to you as a child? Well, these little devils are not those cookies. I have infused these holiday treats with the fire to awaken any sleepy palate. They are not unbearably hot; in fact, you won't taste the fire right away. They come at you subtly—first you get the wonderful taste of ginger and spices, then the fire grows; yes, these are gingerbread bikers from hell. They are not for little kids, but they will bring out the little kid in you.

4 tablespoons (½ stick) unsalted butter, softened

¾ cup sugar

1 extra-large egg plus 1 yolk

¼ cup dark molasses

½ teaspoon ground cloves

½ teaspoon ground nutmeg

½ teaspoon ground allspice

2 teaspoons ground cinnamon

2 teaspoons ground ginger

1 teaspoon ground cayenne pepper

1 teaspoon vanilla extract

2 tablespoons half-and-half or light cream

1½ teaspoons baking soda

3 to 4 cups all-purpose flour

Preheat the oven to 350°F.

Put the butter in a large mixing bowl and blend in the sugar ¼ cup at a time until the mixture is smooth and creamy. Add the egg and egg yolk and the molasses. Blend for 1 minute, or until the mixture is a uniform color and free of lumps. Add the spices, vanilla, cream, and baking soda and mix for 1 minute, or until the spices are fully blended.

Stir in the flour 1 cup at a time until 3 cups have been added. The dough should be stiff and not sticky; to test the dough, form a small piece into a ball and roll it between two pieces of waxed paper. If the

batter sticks to the waxed paper, blend in ¼ cup flour and test again, repeating until you achieve the right consistency.

Form a piece of dough into a cylinder and flatten it slightly between your hands. Place the dough between two sheets of waxed paper and roll it out until it is ¼ inch thick. Peel the top piece of waxed paper off the dough and replace it with a piece of baking parchment. Flip the dough over and peel away the other piece of waxed paper. Use cookie cutters or cut the dough freehand with a sharp knife.

The cookies will expand slightly during baking, so leave ¼ to ½ inch between them. Remove the excess dough. Reroll the scraps and cut more cookies. Place the sheet of baking parchment containing the cut cookies on a cookie sheet and bake for 8 to 10 minutes. Allow the cookies to cool slightly before removing from the baking sheet.

When cool, decorate the cookies with colored icing. Serve them immediately or store in a sealed container. These cookies will keep well, but they harden. Placing a piece of apple in the container with the cookies a day before serving will soften them.

MAKES 4 DOZEN COOKIES

Ballistic Bananas*

Bananas are not one of the first things to come to mind in a discussion of hot foods, but this hot-rod dessert will convince you otherwise. John Dalmas hit the mark with his Viewer Recipe Contest ingredient suggestion of bananas. I love a fun challenge, and this was just the thing, a chance to put the fire where you would least expect it. Just add these to your next banana splits and watch your tongue burn rubber to get to the ice cream.

> **3 tablespoons unsalted butter**
> **1 fresh habanero pepper, stemmed, seeded, and halved**
> **4 ripe bananas, peeled and halved lengthwise**

In a large sauté pan, melt the butter over medium heat. Add the habanero and sauté for 1 minute. Add the bananas and sauté for 2 to 4 minutes, or until they begin to brown. Turn the bananas over and sauté on the other side. While the bananas are sautéing, move the habanero pieces around them; this will help make them all equally ballistic.

Discard the habanero and serve warm with some whipped cream or ice cream as a counterpoint to the fire in the bananas.

MAKES 4 SERVINGS

* Contest winner

Crepes Happen Dessert

If you spend enough time riding or cooking, sooner or later something comes along to make you say "Crepes happen." In this case it's a sinfully good dessert. This recipe takes a little time, but the results are killer.

The recipe has three basic steps. First you prepare the batter, then, while the batter is resting, you fix the sauce. Finally, when the sauce is almost finished, you fry up the crepes, and everything is ready for assembly. The whole process takes about $1\frac{1}{2}$ hours, but it is an easy dessert.

BATTER

1 cup all-purpose flour
$\frac{1}{8}$ teaspoon salt
3 large eggs
$1\frac{1}{2}$ cups milk
2 tablespoons oil

SAUCE

12 ounces frozen cherries, or 2 cups fresh, pitted
$\frac{1}{2}$ cup honey
$\frac{1}{2}$ cup water
1 fresh habanero pepper, stemmed, seeded, and halved
$\frac{1}{2}$ cup half-and-half
$\frac{1}{2}$ cup chocolate chips

Butter, for frying
Confectioners' sugar

To prepare the batter: Combine the ingredients for the batter in a large bowl and mix with a wire whisk until very smooth. (This can also be

done in a blender or a food processor.) Refrigerate for 1 hour in a tightly covered container.

To prepare the sauce: In a medium saucepan, combine the cherries, honey, water, and habanero pepper. Place over medium heat and bring to a boil. Reduce the heat to low and simmer for 30 minutes.

Remove the saucepan from the heat and stir in the half-and-half. Transfer the cherry mixture to a blender and puree until smooth. Return to the saucepan and place over very low heat. Add the chocolate chips and stir until they are melted and well blended into the sauce. Keep warm.

To assemble the crepes: In a medium cast-iron frying pan over moderately high heat, melt enough butter to coat the pan. Pour ¼ cup of the batter into the pan and immediately swirl the batter around to form a thin pancake. Fry for 30 seconds to 1 minute, or until the batter is firm and the edges start to brown. Turn the pancake over and fry the other side for 30 seconds to 1 minute. Place the cooked pancake on a plate and keep warm by covering with an inverted plate or a dish towel. Repeat until all the pancakes are cooked.

Lay a crepe on a plate. Spread on several spoonfuls of the sauce and roll the crepe up. Drizzle a little sauce over the rolled crepe and sprinkle with some confectioners' sugar. Repeat with the remaining crepes.

MAKES 12 TO 16 CREPES

NOTE: As a variation, place some fresh fruit pieces on the crepe, then roll it up.

Blender Blaster Pie

I love cheesecake. I know this little cheesecake place in the mountains that I will ride over a hundred miles to get to, just for a slice (or two). But I can save you the trip—this is a faux cheesecake that is as close as your freezer. You see, it is "baked" in the freezer. The recipe is so simple and tastes so good that the hardest part is waiting for it to freeze. I have developed this pie with a special twist—the sauce holds the fire. The pie is just rich and sweet, but the sauce is sweet and hot.

CRUST

8 ounces graham crackers, crumbled (1½ cups)
½ cup confectioners' sugar
½ cup (1 stick) lightly salted butter, melted

FILLING

¼ cup light cream
¼ cup chocolate syrup
¼ cup sour cream
8 ounces cream cheese, cut into 8 pieces
½ cup confectioners' sugar

SAUCE

½ fresh habanero pepper, stemmed and seeded
¼ cup honey
1 pint fresh strawberries

To prepare the crust: Combine the graham cracker crumbs and confectioners' sugar in a blender or food processor. Pulse several times un-

til the crumbs are reduced to a coarse grain. Add the melted butter a little at a time, pulsing after each addition. (It may be necessary to scrape down the sides of the blender between additions of butter.) After all the butter has been added, pulse several times to combine. To test the mixture to see if it is fully combined, pinch a small amount with your fingers; if it holds together, it is ready to use.

Spread the crust mixture evenly on the bottom and sides of a 9-inch pie pan. Using your fingers or a spoon, pack the crumbs firmly to form a solid crust. Chill the crust in the refrigerator for 15 to 30 minutes.

To prepare the filling: In a blender or food processor, combine the cream, chocolate syrup, and sour cream. Blend for 30 seconds, or until the mixture is a smooth, even chocolate color. Add the cream cheese one piece at a time, pulsing once or twice after each addition. When all the cream cheese has been added, blend on low for 30 seconds. Add the confectioners' sugar and blend at the lowest speed for 1 minute, or until the mixture is smooth. Set aside.

To prepare the sauce: Chop the habanero in a blender. Add the honey and blend on low for 1 minute. Reserve 2 to 4 good-looking strawberries for the top and add the rest to the blender a few at a time, pulsing once or twice after each addition. When all of the strawberries have been added, blend for 30 seconds at low speed. Refrigerate, covered, until chilled, about 1 hour.

To assemble the pie: Pour the filling into the crust. Cover with waxed paper and place in the freezer for 4 hours, or until the center of the pie does not wiggle when you shake the pan gently. Just before serving, halve the reserved strawberries. Cut the pie into slices while it is still frozen and top each slice with a strawberry half. Serve with the sauce ladled around the strawberry and, if you like, a swirl of chocolate syrup on top.

MAKES ONE 9-INCH PIE OR 4 TO 6 TARTS

NOTE: As an alternative you can make 4 to 6 small tarts with these ingredients. Try this when you want to serve the pie without waiting so long to freeze it. You can chill the crusts while you prepare the filling and sauce.

Sources

BIKER BILLY COOKS WITH FIRE
P.O. Box 1888
Weaverville, NC 28787
www.bikerbilly.com
bikerbilly@bikerbilly.com
Event and appearance information,
newsletter, Biker Billy products, and
fiery stuff

CHILE PEPPER MAGAZINE
1701 River Run Suite #901
Fort Worth, TX 76107
888-774-2946
www.chilepepper.com
The magazine of spicy world cuisine

PENDERY'S
1221 Manufacturing Street
Dallas, TX 75207
800-533-1870
www.penderys.com
Fiery foods and products

KALUSTYAN'S
123 Lexington Avenue
New York, NY 10016
212-685-3888
www.kalustyans.com
Indian & Middle Eastern spices and foods

W. ATLEE BURPEE & CO.
300 Park Avenue
Warminster, PA 18974
800-888-1447
www.burpee.com
Everything a gardner needs including
Biker Billy Hybrid Hot Pepper seeds

SHEPHERD'S GARDEN SEEDS
P.O. Box 50, Route 63
Litchfield, Connecticut 06759
800-503-9624
www.whiteflowerfarm.com
Hot pepper seeds

TOMATO GROWERS SUPPLY COMPANY
P.O. Box 2237
Fort Myers, FL 33902
888-478-7333
www.tomatogrowers.com
Hot pepper seeds

AMA (AMERICAN MOTORCYCLIST ASSOCIATION)
13515 Yarmouth Drive
Pickerington, OH 43147
800-AMA-JOIN
800-262-5646
www.amadirectlink.com
National organization defending motorcycle rights; also sanctions clubs, events,
and races

DISCOVER TODAY'S MOTORCYCLING
2 Jenner Street
Suite 150
Irvine, CA 92718
949-727-4211
www.motorcycles.org
Provides information about motorcycling and how to get started. Call 800-
833-3995 to receive four free
brochures–*Straight Facts: Prepare to Ride,
How to Insure, What to Buy, How to
Finance.*

MOTORCYCLE SAFETY FOUNDATION
2 Jenner Street
Suite 150
Irvine, CA 92718
949-727-3227
www.mfs-usa.org
Designs, supports, and certifies rider-
education programs. For the nearest
class call 800-447-4700.

MOTORCYCLE RIDERS FOUNDATION
P.O. Box 1808
Washington, D.C. 20013
202-546-5894
www.mrf.org
Washington, DC-based grass-roots
organization supported by and support-
ing state motorcycle rights organizations
(MROs). Can provide referrals to your
local state MRO.

MOTORCYCLE SAFETY FOUNDATION

The Motorcycle Safety Foundation is a national, nonprofit organization promoting the safety of motorcyclists with programs in rider training, operator licensing, and public information. Since its inception in 1973, the foundation has supported state and independent programs in training one million students to ride more safely.

Training one million riders is a major milestone in motorcycle safety, especially since it was a private initiative with industry funding on a voluntary basis. The Motorcycle Safety Foundation is sponsored by the U.S. distributors of Honda, Suzuki, Kawasaki, Yamaha, and BMW motorcycles.

Take an MSF RiderCourse® by calling 1-800-447-4700 for the Straight Facts brochures and for the location of the RiderCourse® nearest you.

Always wear protective gear:
- helmet
- over-the-ankle boots

247

- gloves
- goggles/face shield
- long pants
- long-sleeved shirt/jacket

Read your owner's manual and prepare your vehicle.

Know your limitations:
- Personal
- Vehicle
- Environment

Know the state and local laws.

Ride aware—avoid accidents and injury.

Don't drink and ride.

Index

Acknowledgments

THE PROCESS of writing a cookbook is very much like riding a long motorcycle adventure. You and your bike start from one point with a planned route and a feeling of excitement about the road to come. Along the way you meet new people and discover byways that no map can reveal. And, at the ride's end you realize that the true joy of adventure lies within the new people you meet, the new things you learn, and the unexpected experiences that await you around every bend of the road.

There are many people I would like to thank for their contributions to this book. I would like to start by thanking someone who taught me more than I could ever realize—my mom, Gladys Hufnagle. She always believed in me and allowed me to be myself. Her independence and positive approach to life was a great influence on me. Raising me by herself after my father died was more than enough work for two people, but she never let it show. She did show me, by her example, that I could do anything if I tried. I only wish she had lived to see this book.

When you learn to ride a motorcycle it is very important to work with instructors who love the sport and are willing to give you the time, help, and encouragement that are critical to success. Gasper Trama and his whole team at Trama Auto School gave me those things and, in doing so, expanded my world. The Motorcycle Safety Foundation and all the people who work tirelessly to support and advance rider education deserve a big Alright! for helping to make riding a motorcycle safer and more enjoyable one rider at a time.

In many ways writing this book has also been a lot like learning to ride. I have again been blessed with a team that has given me the help and encouragement to make my dream a reality. Special thanks are due my editor, Megan Newman, whose encouragement and guidance have made her a cherished "traveling companion" on this road.

This book is part of my journey, along which there are many people who have provided help, advice, love, inspiration, comfort, and companionship. I would like to especially thank them. However, there is not enough paper to list the names of all my friends and riding companions whose support and confidence mean so much to me, so let me just say, Alright!

I would also like to thank all the people who tested recipes; this includes the Morris County Chapter of United ABATE of New Jersey, my friends from Chapter NJB of the GWRRA, and the many other hungry bikers who volunteered to taste the fire.

And then there are the pictures—what road trip is complete without photos? First let me thank Brian Smale and his pyrotechnic crew for capturing the fire for the cover. Special thanks go to the friends who shared their family albums of motorcycle memories: Joe Allen, Dick Brock, Bob Denecke, the Hefele family, Frank Leonard, Brian Rathjen, and Dave "Desh" Shaw. A big thanks goes to Harley-Davidson, Inc., for providing some "factory photos," and for building the stuff biker dreams are made of.

Warm thanks to good friend Beau Allen Pacheco for his kind thoughts in the Foreword. I would also like to thank Jack Savage and the team at Whitehorse along with my literary agent James Fitzgerald for making this new paperback edition possible. Their efforts make it possible to share this book and it's fiery delights with many new readers, cooks and friends. Sharing the fire with all of you makes me want to holler: Alright, Eat Hot, Ride Safe and Cook With Fire!